First edition, September, 1982.
Second Edition, January, 1982

Published by

Prelude Press
Box 69773
Los Angeles, California
90069

Distributed by Ballantine Books,
a division of Random House, Inc.
201 East 50th Street
New York, New York
10022

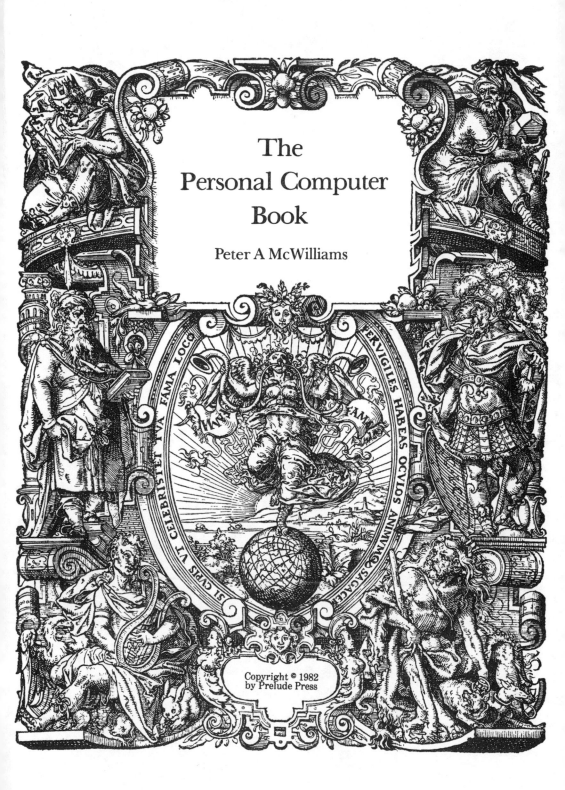

The
Personal Computer
Book

Peter A McWilliams

CONTENTS

PART II

THE USES OF
PERSONAL COMPUTERS

PART III

SELECTING AND PURCHASING A PERSONAL COMPUTER

For Fran Howell

with gratitude.

The
Personal Computer
Book

Introduction

This is a book for people who know little or nothing about computers, personal or otherwise.

It's for people who have had their curiosity piqued by the televised endorsement of computers by such diverse personalities as Dick Cavett, George Plimpton, and Charlie Chaplin. It is a book for those who, watching these commercials, have asked themselves, "Dick Cavett?" "George Plimpton?" "*Charlie Chaplin?*"

It's a book for those who wonder what personal computers are, what they have to offer, and what these offerings will cost.

It's for people who have had their "computer literacy" questioned by such literary giants as *Time*, *Newsweek*, and *People*.

It's for people who don't know the difference between a microprocessor and a microorganism — who think a "Pac-Man" is a member of the Sierra Club.

Finally, and most importantly, it is a book for people who aren't all that serious about the whole computer thing. I am reminded of the late Alan Watts, who said that he was not *serious* about his work, but that he was *sincere*. I am sincere in my admiration of personal computers as powerful tools, and I am sincerely amused by those who take these tools too seriously.

In researching this book, it was necessary to attempt reading the other introductory books on personal computers. One claimed that computers were the most important invention since fire, or perhaps the wheel. I only got through three or four more pages of that book. Another said that computers were the most important step, evolutionwise, since our ancestors jumped out of the trees. I stopped reading that one right there.

Having, in my own haphazard way, studied computers for three years — and having owned a personal computer for two — I find it difficult to accept as a guide anyone that *serious* about computers.

In this book I will do my best to be a sincere guide, though not a serious one.

If I were to look upon the time line of humanity, and were asked to locate an evolutionary turning point that most closely resembles the advent of personal computers, I wouldn't have to go back any farther than thirty years — the popular acceptance of television. Television was successfully demonstrated in 1927 and made commercially available in 1941, but it wasn't until the late 1940s and early 1950s that television became truly popular. (In 1946 there were 10,000 TVs in the United States. By 1951 there were 12,000,000. In 1958 — 50,000,000.)

Few will deny the impact television has made upon the United States and most of the industrialized world. Observing us coolly from North of the border, Canadian philosopher Marshall McLuhan noted that the world had become a global village.

I do not think, however, that television rates the same niche in the evolution of the species as fire or learning to walk on two legs. Nor do personal computers.

As with all the technological advances of the last hundred years — typewriters, telephones, electric lights, phonographs, automobiles, airplanes, movies, radio, television — personal computers will change our lives, and our lives will change them.

In some areas, personal computers will prove so invaluable that they will soon be considered a necessity — small businesses for example. Big business simply could not continue without their big computers. (It is estimated that duplicating the daily output of all the large computers in the world would require three *trillion* clerical workers.)

Word processing, accounting, cost projections, inventory control, and similar functions are handled so swiftly and effortlessly by personal computers that, within a few years, the small businessperson will be as addicted to small computers as the big businessperson is addicted to the big. (See the chapter on *Personal Computers in Business*.)

In other areas, personal computers will prove so unnecessary as to be considered a nuisance — reading the daily newspaper, scheduling appointments, filing personal income taxes, locking the doors at night, or turning the coffee on in the morning. (See Chapter Ten, *What Personal Computers Do Not Do Well.*)

In most areas, however, true to its name, the value of a personal computer will depend upon the personal interests of the person using the computer. Personal computers play games — from chess to Missile Command —better than anything else around. But you must fancy games. They will chart your biorhythms with great accuracy. But you must care to know what your biorhythms are. Using a telephone to plug into a large computer, you can research any subject imaginable. But first, you must have something to research.

For the most part, personal computers will prove their worth to the degree that they fit into your daily life, not to the degree that you adapt your life to be more in step with The Computer Age.

In this book, we'll explore the things that personal computers do — the things they do well and the things they don't do well. You can decide if any of these accomplishments warrant inviting this latest prodigy of the industrial revolution into your home or office.

COMPUTERS BY BALLOON.

"Well, of course I love you.
But a personal computer is forever."

PART I

What Personal Computers Are and What They Do

Chapter One

The Personal Computer

Before exploring what these E.Ts. called P.Cs. do, let's take a look at what they *are*.

Like most machines, personal computers are made up of metal, glass, paper, and plastic — with an occasional exotic-sounding substance like phosphorus thrown in for good measure.

If you feel intimidated by computers, there's no need to be. They are constructed of the same bits and pieces as televisions, typewriters, and tape recorders.

This chapter will provide a general overview of a personal computer's component parts. We'll go into more detail, from a buyer's point of view, in a later chapter, *Selecting a Personal Computer*.

As we go along, I will also introduce you — as painlessly as possible — to that collection of jargon, technical terms, and buzz words known as **Computerese**. There's nothing to be intimidated about here, either. The people who created Computerese are far less intelligent than you. How do I know they are far less intelligent than you? Because, considering the mishmash of tortured conjunctions and fractured idioms they have jumbled together, it's obvious that they are far less intelligent than anyone.

And so, with intimidation on hold, heads held high, and a song in our hearts, let's take a look at the bits and pieces that make up a personal computer.

The first bit of the personal computer we'll look at is the **microprocessor**. A processor in *any* computer does just that: it **processes** information. It sorts and resorts bits of information, something almost any human could do, but it sorts and resorts at speeds no human can approach. It is this speed, not any innate ability, that give computers the edge over humans in certain repetitive tasks.

In a larger computer, the processor can be any size at all. A large corporation can simply lease another floor to put it on. In a personal computer, a processor can be only so large or it stops being a personal computer and

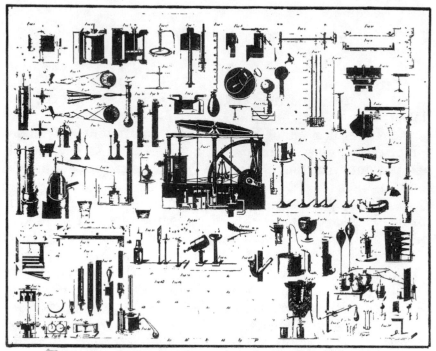

The component parts of a personal computer (PLATE 1).

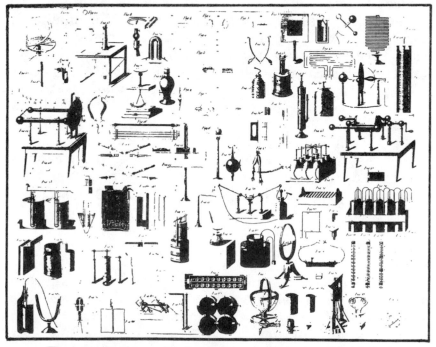

The component parts of a personal computer (PLATE 2).

becomes a coffee table. Once processors became small enough they were dubbed *micro*processors. (In the world of electronics, when something is made small it is prefaced with *mini*. When it is made smaller it is prefaced by *micro*, and when it is made smaller still, by *mini-micro*. I am sure before the decade is out we will see *micro-micros*, *mini-micro-micros*, and *micro-micro-micros*.)

Some microprocessors are basic affairs, designed for a specific function within a specific product. A microprocessor inside a hand-held calculator, for example, may be constructed to simply add, subtract, tell the time, and play a heart rending version of *Clair de lune*.

By the time they mature enough to be included in a personal computer, microprocessors assume the more sophisticated name of **Central Processing Unit**, which is usually shortened to the not-so-sophisticated **CPU**.

Microprocessors are made of silicon. Silicon is a fancy word for glass. (Not to be confused with *silicone*, a fancy word for rubber.) It's called silicon because it is made from silica, a fancy word for sand.

It has been said that the meek shall inherit the earth. Remember those meek little math students, running around high school with slide rules and pencils sticking out of their shirt pockets, the ones the jocks labeled nerds, the ones who never dated because (a) no one would date them and (b) they were always in the basement working on their science project? Well, those meek have inherited the earth, the sand to be specific, silica to be more specific.

They have inherited, too, a chunk of actual earth in California called Silicon Valley (not to be confused with Silicone Valley, a section of Beverly Hills reserved for plastic surgeons and their more affluent clients). In Silicon Valley the nerds have become rich with their science projects, and the former-jocks all over the country are trying to save enough money to buy one of these mass-produced projects for their children.

A microprocessor is very smart but has very little memory, rather like a genius with amnesia. To remedy this situation, two kinds of memory are combined with the Central Processing Unit in most personal computers.

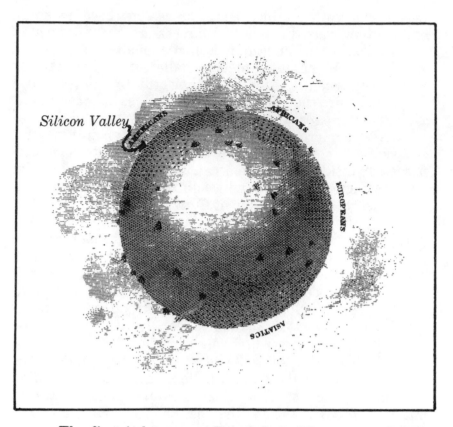

The first is known as **Read Only Memory** or **ROM**. This memory can be "read" by the microprocessor, but the microprocessor cannot "write" anything onto that memory. (*Reading*, meaning taking information from, and *writing*, meaning adding information to, are computerdom's token nods to a form of literacy other than computer literacy.) The microprocessor, then, is free to take information *from* ROM but it cannot add information *to* it.

The information in ROM is placed there — permanently — by the manufacturer. ROM is there like a helpful nurse, telling the amnesia-bound genius how to brush his teeth, get dressed, and otherwise prepare for the day. When electrical current first passes through the CPU, it will wake up and ask ROM, "What do I do now?" ROM will tell it, CPU will do it, and then ask, "What do I do now?" ROM will tell it, CPU will do it, and so on. ROM is, in other words, **programmed** to get CPU going in the morning and to maintain certain basic functions during the day.

At a certain point, however, CPU will have done everything ROM has been programmed to ask it to do. CPU is washed, dressed, and ready for the day — but what will that day consist of? CPU asks ROM, "What do I do now?" and ROM replies, "Ask RAM."

RAM is the second kind of memory in a personal computer. RAM stands for **Random Access Memory**. With RAM, not only can CPU read information from RAM, but it can also write information on it. It has random access to that memory; can erase it — or any part of it — and write some more.

RAM is also referred to as **User Programmable Memory**. This means that the user (you or I) can "program in" whatever we want the CPU to do. (We'll discuss programming a computer in Chapter Three. For now, know that programming RAM is as easy as playing a record on a phonograph.)

The CPU turns to RAM and asks, "What do I do now?" RAM has the daily schedule from the Big Boss (you) in hand. "During the morning it's accounting," says RAM, "This afternoon word processing, and in the evening we have scheduled a series of intriguing electronic games." "Right," says CPU, and the three of them — RAM, ROM, and CPU — set off for a productive day.

RAM can be thought of as an executive secretary who has not only the daily schedule, but also a steno pad. If CPU were to ask ROM to take a note, ROM would reply, "That's not my job. Ask RAM." RAM is more than happy to jot down anything from a telephone number to a telephone book, and to have that information ready for the CPU's use at a nanosecond's notice.

RAM is obviously a more versatile servant to CPU than ROM, but RAM, alas, has a memory problem of its own. As long as electrical current is flowing through its little brain, RAM remembers everything. Once the current is withdrawn, RAM forgets it all. (ROM, on the other hand, remembers how to get CPU up and dressed, current or no current, indefinitely.) Every time a computer is turned

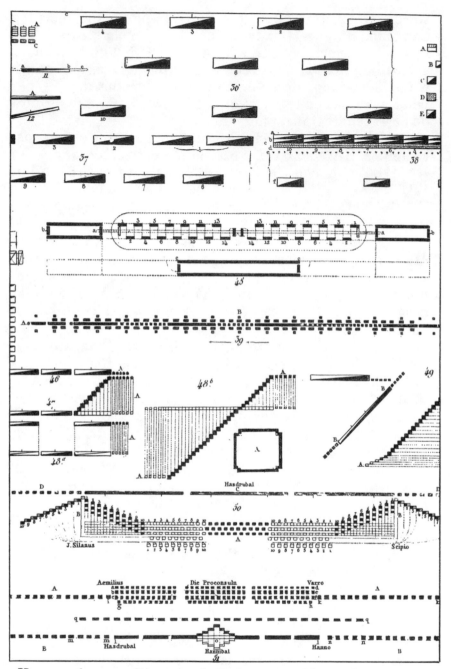

Here we have a diagram of the inner workings of a personal computer.

off, it's a blank tabula rasa for RAM.

There must be a way, then, to (a) save the information in RAM before turning the power off and (b) loading information back into RAM after turning the power back on. That way is either cartridges or magnetic media.

Cartridges look like 8-track tapes and plug into the computer. These can either be game playing cartridges (a different game or set of games on each cartridge), or more "serious" applications — a checkbook cartridge, for example, might keep a running balance of how overdrawn you are.

Magnetic media for personal computers come in two types, tapes and disks. The tapes used are of the standard cassette variety, the same kind you'll find in $4,000 audiophile tape decks, $100 Sony Walkmans, and $19.95 cassette players from K Mart.

Disks are either 5¼- or 8-inch circles of plastic covered with the same brown stuff that is found on cassettes. (The brown stuff, by the way, is rust; ordinary garden-hoe variety rust. Naturally, no one would want to pay $5 for a piece of plastic covered with rust, so the rust is known as "iron oxide.") These thin circles are permanently enclosed in a cardboard envelope to protect them from dust, dirt, and sticky fingers. These disks are also known as **floppy disks**, **minidisks**, and **diskettes**.

Cassettes require nothing more elaborate than the aforementioned $19.95 K Mart cassette player and some sort of interface to work with a personal computer. (An **interface** is any device that lets one device work with another device. Clear?)

Disks require a special player known as a **disk drive**. A disk goes into a disk drive, protective covering and all. There, the inner plastic circle is rotated at several hundred rotations per minute, while a record/playback head moves across the disk's surface. These heads are known as **read/write heads**. Information is read from the disk and written on the disk by them. Most drives have one read/write head, unless it is a **double sided** disk drive, in which case it would have two heads — rather like the old juke boxes that could play either side of a vertically spinning record.

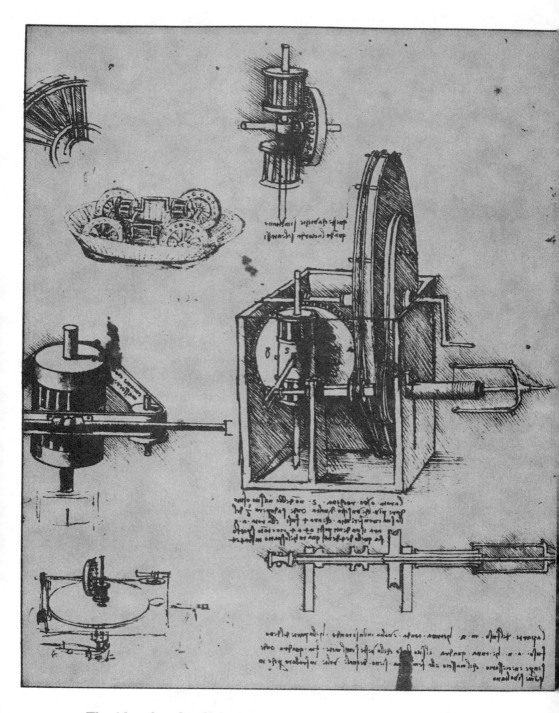

The idea for the disk drive is not new. Here are Leonardo da Vinci's sketches for a manually operated disk drive, circa 1490.

Larrilyn

Chris EGAN

Investment Clothier

464-2210

Ron

1-10

QS:119

GA

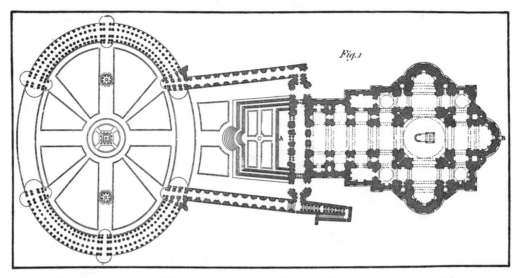

Fig. 1

Michelangelo tried to improve upon Leonardo's design by making the disks oval ("More esthetically pleasing," Michelangelo wrote in his journal). Leonardo, in Florence, sent a terse note to the young sculptor in Rome: "Whatsa matta you?" Leonardo wrote, "The diska drive, shesa my idea. You keepa you hands off." Michelangelo eventually found another use for his design.

Early disk drives required one full horsepower to operate.

How information is stored on disks: Here we have the disk for the video game "A Weekend in the Country." As you can see, everything is made small so it can fit.

Cassette players, as you may have surmised, are less expensive than disk drives. Cassettes are, however, much slower and far more prone to error. (We'll discuss cassettes vs. disks further in the chapter on *Selecting a Personal Computer.*)

Another kind of magnetic media becoming more and more popular with personal computers, especially personal computers used for business applications, are **hard disks.** Hard disks operate very much like floppy disks. The difference between a floppy disk and a hard disk is that the hard disk is made of metal, not plastic; it spins at a much faster speed; it holds five to fifty times more information; it reads and writes faster; and, of course, it costs more. Whereas floppy disks are changeable, hard disks (usually) are not.

With magnetic media we have a way of getting information into RAM when we turn the computer on, and a way to store information from RAM before we turn the computer off. But how do we get in and fiddle around with the information in between times? What we need are some **input devices.** That's where keyboards and joysticks come in.

A **keyboard** is a board with keys on it, looking very much like the keyboard on a typewriter. Each key represents a letter or a number or a bit of punctuation or a symbol of some kind.

Inexpensive personal computers use **membrane keyboards.** These are flat membranes of rubbery plastic with the keys printed on the surface. When the rubbery plastic is depressed and electrical contact is made just below its surface, a keystroke is recorded.

Less inexpensive personal computers ($300 and up, in most cases) use mechanical keyboards that more closely resemble the action of a typewriter. Each letter, number, or symbol has its own plastic key. This key is attached to an electrical switch. Each time a key is depressed, contact is made, and a keystroke is registered. Mechanical keyboards are much easier to use than are the membrane variety.

With a keyboard, almost anything can be communicated to a computer. Words, numbers, symbols, which way the spaceship should go, when it should fire, and so on. Even graphics can be communicated through the keyboard. (A device known as a **light pen** can also be used. This allows one to draw on the computer screen just as though it were chalk on a chalkboard.)

Serious game players, however, will require a **joystick**. A joystick is a little box one holds in one's hand. A stick protrudes from this box, as do one or more buttons. If one pushes the stick up, the spaceship (or submarine or boxer or chess piece) moves up the screen. When the stick is pushed down, the spaceship *et al* moves down. The same is true of right, left, diagonals, and circles.

When the button is pushed, a missile is fired (or a torpedo is launched, or a punch is thrown, or a move is finalized). All this stick moving and button pushing has been observed to create the emotion of Joy in certain humans, hence the term joystick.

Input devices — keyboards and joysticks — get information into the computer. How do you suppose we get information out? You guessed it: **output devices**. These include video screens and printers.

The **video screen** on a personal computer looks just like the screen on a television set — in fact, the video screen on some personal computers actually *is* a television set. A wire connects the personal computer to the antenna of a television and the computer literally broadcasts a signal to the TV.

A video screen is also known as a **CRT**, which stands for cathode ray tube, which is the kind of tube a TV picture tube really is.

The video screen (or **video display**) of more sophisticated personal computers is not a computer-by-day and a television-by-night. These video screens are known as **monitors** and are connected directly to the computer. Monitors display better images than do moonlighting televisions.

The display can be either in color or **monochrome**. Monochrome simply means "one color." Monochrome colors for personal computers are green (dark green background with lighter green lettering), amber (dark amber background with lighter amber — almost yellow — lettering), and the ever popular white (white lettering against a basic black background.) Most computers allow the screen display to be reversed so that dark characters can appear against light backgrounds.

Color video is everywhere. We're so used to seeing color when we look at a video screen that some advertising agencies, in yet another desperate attempt to attract our attention, are now producing television commercials in black & white. For games, graphics, and the education of younger children, color video is certainly the way to go. For words and numbers, however, monochrome displays offer sharper character display.

Video displays are ephemeral. Like RAM, once the power is turned off, the video screen forgets. A more permanent method of "outputting" information is found in the **printer**. A printer, naturally, prints things.

A printer is known as a **peripheral**. It is so named because it is peripheral to the use of the computer — useful, but not necessary. At one time, almost everything other than CPU, ROM, and RAM were considered peripherals. As personal computers have gotten more sophisticated, the line between "the computer" and "its peripherals" has blurred. Is a disk drive a peripheral? A keyboard? A joystick? People have differing opinions. Most people do, however, draw the line at printers. (An "all in one" personal computer might include everything we've discussed thus far, but would not include a printer.)

There are two kinds of printers, dot matrix and letter quality. **Dot matrix** printers form characters with little dots, very much like the signs on banks that tell the time and temperature. Dot matrix printers are not the greatest for correspondence, but are necessary for intricate graphics.

For correspondence (letters, reports, and such) one would need a **letter quality** printer. These print a bit slower and cost a bit more than their dot matrix cousins, but the quality of their type rivals that of electric typewriters. This is because, in a very real sense, they *are* electric typewriters. They type one character after another, just like a typewriter. Printers made especially for computers are constructed for continual full-tilt use, something most typewriters are not. Further, computer printers are designed to use some features not generally available on typewriters, such as boldface printing.

Another popular peripheral for the personal computer is known as a **modem**. A modem attaches to the computer and to a telephone. It allows one computer to be connected, over phone lines, to another computer. (The other computer requires a modem as well.) When connected, information can flow back and forth between computers.

The process modems use to transmit computer information over ordinary phone lines is called *modulation.* (Modulation also takes place with information before it can be broadcast over the airwaves. The "M" in AM and FM radio stands for modulation.)

A modem takes information from the computer, modulates it, and sends it over the phone line. A second modem at the other end *de*modulates the signal back into a form the receiving computer can understand. "Mo-dem," then, describes what a modem does — *mo*dulate/*dem*odulate.

A modem puts your computer in touch with the world. We'll discuss the practical benefits of this ability at various points throughout the book, especially chapter four.

And there we have it — the personal computer. How they work and where they came from is discussed in the next chapter. What they do is discussed in Part II. How to select and purchase one is the subject of Part III.

In the 1920s, this was one of radio's most popular "peripherals."
Prior to the loudspeaker, all listening had to be done through
headphones. Considering its potential, personal computing is about
where radio was in the early 1920s.

Making phosphor.

Chapter Two

An Incomplete and No Doubt Inaccurate History of Personal Computers Including Some Basic Information on How They Work

Boy, I sure wish I had Mr. Wizard to help me with this chapter. Somehow Mr. Wizard made "the magic and mystery of science" understandable and, even when it wasn't understandable, at least it was fun.

If this were television, there would be a shot of me, leaning pensively on the edge of my keyboard, saying "Boy, I sure wish I had Mr. Wizard to help me with this chapter," and suddenly Don Herbert would appear, maybe in a white lab coat, maybe in a suit, and I would become Everyperson and he would become Mr. Wizard, and tell us all about how computers work.

Alas, this is not television, this is a book, and nothing appears suddenly during the writing of a book other than creditors. If this book ever becomes a TV show, maybe the budget will permit Mr. Wizard to join us.

It would be nice to have Sir Kenneth Clark of *Civilization* stop by, too. Lord Clark could show us, through the sketches of Michelangelo and the paintings of the Louvre, how computing has developed through the ages. *Computization* we'll call it. Besides, it's always good to have a "Sir" on the show.

Until that time we'll muddle through on our own, knowing that somewhere, somebody must know how to make all this stuff clear.

This is an optional chapter. You will never need to know *how* computers work. All you need to know is *that* they work. (They do.)

Somewhere along the line you may want to learn how to *operate* a computer, but that is very different from how a computer operates. How a computer operates is of no practical value whatsoever — unless you're a computer designer.

Most of the books and articles written about computers have been written by scientists — or worse, by people trying to *sound* like scientists — and what scientists find necessary to know they assume everyone will find necessary to know. We don't.

How many people know how their refrigerator works? Let's have a show of hands. Your cassette tape recorder? Your car? Your houseplants? Your liver? Does it really matter if you don't? All that matters is that you know how to run it, play it, drive it, water it, or leave it blessedly alone so that it can operate as designed, unmolested.

At some point, even the most educated among us must say, "I don't know how it works" to some essential bit of machinery, and somehow that ignorance doesn't stop the machine from working. Somewhere there is an expert who does know how it works — or at least how to fix it — and that's all that's necessary.

And so it is with computers. That there are silicon chips sorting and re-storing billions of binary bits per nanosecond is of no practical concern to the corporate attorney playing Pac-Man or the teenager using a computer to write his first love poem.

The much-used phrase "computer literacy" has little to do with knowing what goes on inside the machine. It has to do with getting what you want *into* the machine and getting what you want *out of* the machine, and feeling comfortable enough about this process of in and out to occasionally enjoy it.

"Turn the machine on, put the record on the turntable, put the needle on the record, and adjust the volume to your taste" is all one needs to know about a phonograph to enjoy everything from Bette Midler to Gustav Mahler.

The fact that sound is made up of vibrations, and that these vibrations are captured in the grooves of the record, and that the needle vibrates when going through those grooves, and that those vibrations when amplified recreate the original vibrations and therefore the sound of the original performance, is not necessary to know.

It can, however, be interesting. A *National Geographic Special* on how the human body works can be fascinating, even though we've been successfully operating our bodies for years without all those microscopic, time-lapsed, animation-enhanced "hows."

And so it is with the hows, as well as the history, of computers. (The hows and the history of most machinery is intimately connected.) What follows are some hows and some history of computing, presented in no particular order and selected because I found each of them for some reason interesting. This is decidedly not a comprehensive overview of the history and internal functioning of computing machines. It's more a collection of computer trivia.

If your eyes begin to glaze or your mind begins to drift during any of these points, don't bother to refocus and reread, just skip to the next point. If you drift on several points, skip to the next chapter. This information is not in the least essential to selecting, purchasing, operating, and enjoying a personal computer. Like all trivia, it can be interesting but it is, in essence, trivial.

• The first computer was the abacus. The abacus is from the Orient, although its name comes from the Greek word abax, meaning a calculating table covered with dust, which was named after the Hebrew word for dust. The abacus is more than 5,000 years old and is still the primary form of "number crunching" in many parts of the world. (Although the 1982 Chinese census was counted on modern computers, the census preceding it was computed on the abacus.)

The abacus is not only one of humankind's first complex machines, it's also the first mechanical device listed in most dictionaries.

• The next major breakthrough in computers came a scant 4,600 years after the invention of the abacus. In 1642, French scientist Blaise Pascal invented an "arithmetic machine" to help in his father's business. (A father's necessity was the mother of this invention.)

The machine had eight wheels, each wheel having the numbers 0 through 9 painted on them. The wheels were attached to gears and the gears attached to each other in such a way that simple addition and subtraction could take place by dialing the amounts to be added or subtracted. Its size made it the world's first non-portable computer.

Blaise Pascal was honored by having a high-level computer language — Pascal — named after him. (I understand that a low-level computer language, Blaise, is in the works.)

• In 1694, 52 long years after Pascal's arithmetic machine, the German mathematician Gottfried Wilhelm Leibniz unveiled his 23-year pet project, the Stepped Reckoner. This machine was designed to not only add and subtract, but to multiply, divide and extract square roots. This was a major advance in features, and there was only one thing wrong with the machine — it didn't work.

It did, however, introduce a new concept to "reckoning," and that was "stepping." The concept was to break a mathematical problem into smaller steps, steps so small that the average human would find following that many steps tedious and time-consuming, but steps that a machine could do rather quickly and without noticeable signs of boredom.

Whereas Pascal used ten symbols in each mathematical problem (0, 1, 2, 3, 4, 5, 6, 7, 8, and 9), Leibniz used only two (0 and 1). The former system is called the decimal system (dec meaning ten) and the latter, binary (bi meaning two).

It is far easier for a machine to keep track of only two variables than for it to keep track of ten. Two variables can be represented in very concrete terms — on/off, yes/no, black/white, in/out, up/down, open/closed.

Absolute, concrete terms are something machines like. The gradation of information that humans enjoy machines don't. It is not surprising that a Frenchman devised a gradation machine (0 through 9 in gradual increments) while a German introduced an absolute machine (0 and 1 and that's that). It would later take an Englishman, George Boole, to massage the Teutonic and the Gallic approaches into the system of logic modern computers would eventually use.

• We all know how the decimal system of numbers works — it's the system of counting we use all the time. We have ten symbols (0, 1, 2, 3, 4, 5, 6, 7, 8, and 9). Whenever we use up all the symbols we must start combining symbols to indicate amounts larger than 9. We do this by columns. The right hand column represents the symbol itself. The column to the left of that represents ten times the value of that symbol. The column to the left of that represents ten times ten, or one-hundred times the number. Each column to the left represents an additional ten-fold increase. (Remember, if you start to drift, move on to the next point. None of this is necessary.)

The first four columns of the decimal system are:

THOUSANDS   HUNDREDS   TENS   ONES

To write "eight" one would put an 8 in the ONES column. To write "eighty," or ten times eight, one would write an 8 in the TENS column and a 0 in the ONES column. The long way of reading that would be "Eight TENS and Zero ONES." (Is anyone besides me having flashbacks of second grade?)

The binary system works in the same way, except that there are only two symbols, 0 and 1. As in decimal, the 0 is used to represent nothing. Therefore, after indicating only *one* variable, the binary system needs a new column. The new column, to the left, indicates a number twice as large as the number in the first column. The next column to the left indicates a number twice as large as the preceding column, and so on.

The first four columns of the binary system would be:

EIGHTS   FOURS   TWOS   ONES

"Eight" in binary would have a 1 in the EIGHTS column, a 0 in the FOURS place, a 0 in the TWOS place and a 0 in the ONES place. The long way of reading that would be, "One EIGHT, zero FOURS, zero TWOS, and zero ONES." It would be written 1000. "8" in decimal equals "1000" in binary.

Before we attempt to represent "eighty" in binary, let's first count from zero to ten in binary.

Zero would be 0. One would be 1. So far so good, but

already we've run out of symbols, so we must add a column to the left. Two would be 10 (one TWO and zero ONES). Three would be 11 (one TWO and one ONE). And again we've run out of symbols. We add an additional column and write 100 (one FOUR, zero TWOS and zero ONES). Five is 101 (one FOUR, zero TWOS, and one ONE). Six is 110 (one FOUR, one TWO, and zero ONES). Seven is 111 (one FOUR, one TWO, and one ONE). Again we've run out of symbols, so we add a column, and return to our old friend 1000 (one EIGHT, zero FOURS, zero TWOS, and zero ONES). Nine is 1001 (one EIGHT, zero FOURS, zero TWOS, and one ONE). Ten is 1010 (one EIGHT, zero FOURS, one TWO, and zero ONES).

To get to "eighty" does not require as many columns as one might think, since each time we add a column to

One of the many distinguished scientists who had nothing whatsoever to do with the development of the computer.

the left it doubles the value of the column immediately to its right. The column to the left of EIGHTS would be SIXTEENS, the column to the left of that THIRTY-TWOS, and the column to the left of that SIXTY-FOURS. It seems that extending the columns this far to the left should give us "eighty."

SIXTY-FOURS THIRTY-TWOS SIXTEENS EIGHTS FOURS TWOS ONES

It becomes sort of a puzzle (the sort of a puzzle which I, by the way, dislike) — "Using a maximum of one number from each column, arrive at the number 'eighty.'"

Let's see, a SIXTY-FOUR and a THIRTY-TWO would give us ninety-six. Over the top already. A SIXTY-FOUR and a SIXTEEN equal — ta-da — eighty. (Boy, did we luck out on that one.) So, we would write "eighty" in binary 1010000 (one SIXTY-FOUR, zero THIRTY-TWOS, one SIXTEEN, zero EIGHTS, zero FOURS, zero TWOS, and zero ONES).

(Challenge: Write the number "twenty-seven" in binary numbers.)

It would seem as though one would require reams of paper to record large numbers in binary. Actually, this is not the case. Because the columns continue to double as they move to the left, the binary system becomes increasingly compact. Whereas it takes seven binary columns to write the decimal number 64 (1000000), it takes only forty binary columns to write the decimal number 549,755,813,888 (10000000000000000000000000000000000000000).

Do you need to know any of this to operate a personal computer? No. None of it. It will, however, help answer the question, "Why are there 64K in the memory of my computer?" Because the Kilobyte ratings of computer memories are usually equal to a binary column number (4K, 8K, 16K, 32K, 64K, 128K, 256K, and so on).

Your computer will accept information in standard decimal form and return processed information in standard decimal form. All conversions to and from binary will take place within the computer.

(Answer to the challenge: "twenty-seven" binary is 11011.)

• A computer is very simple minded. It knows only two things: Yes and No. There are no Maybes. A circuit is either open or it's closed. There is no little-bit-open or almost-closed. It's black or white, no grey whatsoever. It's 0 or 1.

There are two reasons why computers can do all that they do knowing as little as they do.

1. SIZE. A great many yes/no circuits can fit into a very small space. As we saw above, it would take only 40 yes/no circuits to write all numbers from one to one trillion. Computer technology is such that you can hold *millions* of these yes/no circuits in the palm of your hand. This miniaturization allows the computing power of room-sized 1950-computers to fit into the pocket calculators of today. These yes/no circuits are so cheap that you can buy for $100 what would have cost you $1,000,000 thirty years ago.

2. SPEED. One of these little yes/no circuits can say "no" faster than Debbie Boone. Properly induced, it can say "yes" just as fast. This is because each circuit is opened or closed electronically, not mechanically. (There are not millions of little fingers turning millions of little switches on and off.) This means that computers compute at speeds approaching one-fourth the speed of light. In fact, most of the time a computer takes to compute something is in interacting with a mechanical device, such as a disk drive or a joystick.

The speed at which computers operate is so incomprehensible that someone devised this comparison: If you were interacting with a computer — you giving the computer data, the computer giving you data, back and forth — it would take you each time, in the computer's time frame, *eight years* to respond. Having to work as they do with binary numbers and human beings, it is fortunate that computers are not easily bored.

• It was the lack of these two elements, size and speed, that prevented Charles Babbage from constructing a fully-functioning personal computer almost 150 years ago.

By 1835 Babbage, an English inventor, had conceived an "Analytical Engine" that incorporated almost every other element of computing, including programming, memory, printout, and the ever-popular punch cards.

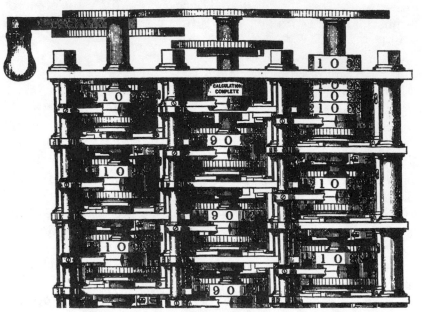

A small portion of Babbage's Analytical Engine.

But Babbage lacked the technology of size and speed, and his 1835 invention of the computer would go unnoticed and forgotten until his writings were rediscovered in 1937.

• Babbage used punch cards borrowed from the Jacquard loom, which Jacquard borrowed from the Vaucanson loom, which Vaucanson borrowed from the Bouchon loom, which Bouchon — the son of an organ maker — borrowed from the automated organ. (This organ to loom to computer connection is delightfully delineated in James Burke's *Connections*, both on the PBS television series and in the Little, Brown and Company book.)

Back in the days of the automated organ (the sixteenth century, give or take a century) a peg was placed on a revolving cylinder for each "yes." As the cylinder turned, the peg would strike a note. This same principle is used in music boxes today.

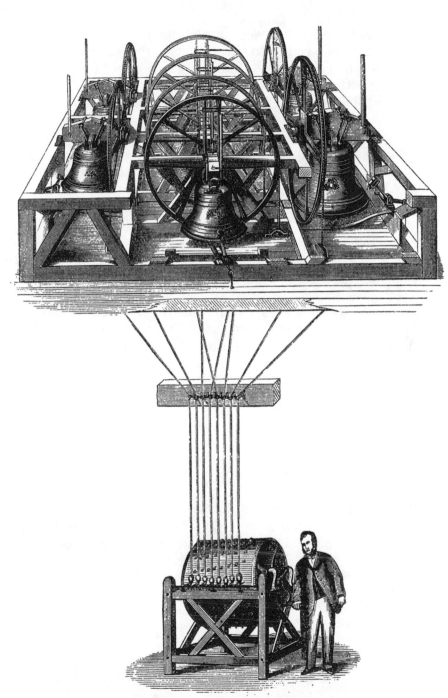

Each time a peg on the drum of this automated bell-ringer pulls a string, the bell attached to that string rings.

The automated weaving looms used paper with holes in it. If a rod could fit in the hole, the thread would be included in the design. If there was no hole for the rod to slip into, the thread would not. This allowed for intricate, inexpensive, and error-free weaving. It's the same concept seen in player piano rolls and computer punch cards.

Punch cards — which until just a few years ago would arrive almost daily in the mail with the ominous warning not to fold, spindle, or mutilate them — work like this:

The card is designed with room to punch out little holes. These holes represent a basic yes/no binary circuit — if the hole is punched, that's yes; if the hole is not punched, that's no. These holes could be assigned to record any answer whatsoever, providing that the answer was either yes or no.

Let's take a very simple punch card that would offer someone the choice of a hot dog, a hamburger, or both. The card would look something like this —

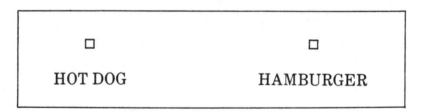

If one wanted a hot dog, he or she would punch-out the hole above hot dog and leave the hamburger hole alone. The "Yes, I want a hot dog; no, I do not want a hamburger" card would look like this —

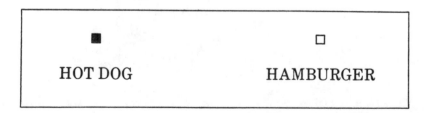

This card would communicate to a computerized kitchen, "I would like a hamburger but not a hot dog":

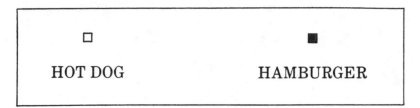

This card would say, "I am obviously hungry. I would like a hot dog *and* a hamburger."

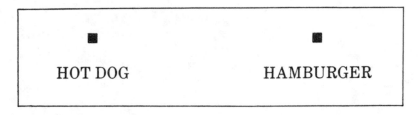

And an unpunched card might mean, "I am on a diet. Do you have any cottage cheese?"

In this way, a card with only two holes has given us four possible choices — hamburger only, hot dog only, hamburger and hot dog, neither hamburger nor hot dog. The choices given the card puncher could be geometrically increased by simply adding a few more holes.

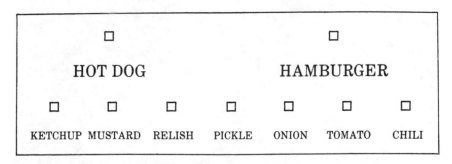

This would offer a range of choices from nothing, to a hamburger *and* a hot dog with everything.

Punch cards, once very popular, have been almost entirely replaced by magnetic disks and tapes. IBM is in the process of recycling billions of these cards. To get some cards for your bird, write IBM, Boca Raton, Florida.

• The 1880 census in the United States took eight years to count. What with the tired and the poor and the huddled masses steaming to America from the teeming shores of Europe, it was estimated that the 1880 census would be counted by 1902. At that rate we would know, by 1985, what the population was in 1930. A better way of counting and sorting was needed and was duly discovered: The 1890 Census Machine.

John Shaw Billings, a medical doctor and lieutenant-colonel in the U.S. Army, came up with the idea of using the punch-hole cards to speed people counting, and turned the project over to Herman Hollerith.

Hollerith designed cards that the census takers could carry with them and punch in the field. The cards included information on sex, age, birth date, nationality — the standard census data. Then the cards were processed by a machine. Each time a hole was in a card, a metal rod would pass through, complete an electrical circuit, and the data was tabulated. However primitive, and although the balance of this computer was purely mechanical, this was the first use of an electric circuit in computing.

The 1890 census was completed, thanks to the computer, in less than three years. In 1911 Hollerith joined with the Computing Tabulating Recording Company, which later became IBM.

• The next two advances came from those hotbeds of progress, war and universities.

By 1939, IBM had become a grand American institution. It joined with another grand American institution, Harvard, and together they made a computer, the Mark I. Partly electrical and partly mechanical, it was the world's largest adding machine. It was fifty feet long and eight feet high. It could add, subtract, multiply, divide, and — most importantly — make mathematical tables. The tables were used by the military in World War II. It told them, for example, where to aim a gun so that the shell and the enemy plane would reach the same place at the same time.

Until WWII, big guns were only asked to fire on stationary objects, like buildings, or on slowly-moving objects, like ships. Airplanes moved at several hundred

The 1890 Census Machine.

miles an hour. The gunner needed to know *exactly* how far in front of the plane to aim. Hence a book of intricate tables was devised that almost required a computer to interpret.

Meanwhile, the University of Pennsylvania, not to be outdone, was working on the first fully electronic computer, the ENIAC (Electronic Numerical Integrator and Calculator). Was this, too, the birth of computer jargon?

The ENIAC took up 3,000 cubic feet (some computer *stores* today are smaller than that), weighed 30 tons, and used 18,000 vacuum tubes. On the average, one tube failed every seven minutes. (When they say that computers today are very reliable, they may be comparing them to the ENIAC.)

The ENIAC was a big hit. When it was first plugged in in 1946 (the year my parents got married — ah, memories) it spent two hours doing nuclear-physics calculations that would have taken 100 engineers one year to compute. How many hours it took ENIAC to come up with *that* statistic we will never know.

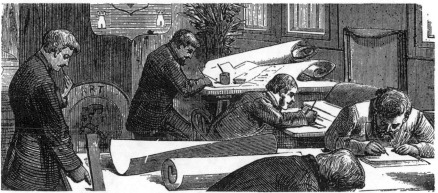

Hard at work, designing the first IBM at Harvard.

● Remington Rand introduced the Univac in 1951. It was the first computer that could handle both numbers *and* letters. The computer was taught to read and write. The first customer in line for the Univac were the folks who started it all back in 1890 — the United States Bureau of Census.

● I love full circles. Here are two more.

Magnetic tape — developed by the Germans during WWII while American computers used paper-punch input to devise gun charts — became the standard storage medium for computers during the 1950s. Those are reels of magnetic tape spinning in the science fiction movies of the period.

The Japanese, still happy with their abacuses, took a neglected invention from the Bell Laboratories — the transistor — and revolutionized the world with it. It began with the transistor radio in the late 1950s and moved to computers in the early 1960s.

Each small, cool, inexpensive, reliable transistor replaced a large, hot, expensive, volatile vacuum tube. Computers became smaller, cooler, less expensive, and more reliable.

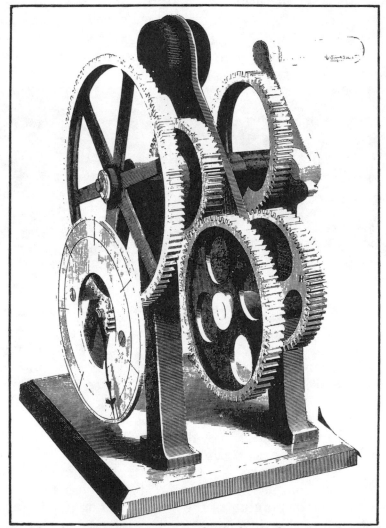

The inside of a transistor as seen through an electron microscope. (SCALE: 1 inch = 4 miles.)

• The late 1960s saw the development of the silicon chip. Each chip, the size of a postage stamp, held the computing power of thousands of transistors, which had replaced thousands of tubes. The ENIAC's 18,000 vacuum tubes and the 30 tons of wiring necessary to connect all those tubes could now fit on a table top.

• The first personal computer was introduced in 1975. The Altair 8800 was a kit offered to hobbyists. It was remarkably — and surprisingly — successful.

Soon the Apple — named after one of its inventor's summer job in an apple orchard — made its debut. It cost $666.66. The Apple was born with a case of the cutes from which it has yet to recover.

Tandy Radio Shack, combining its hobbyist beginnings and its knowledge of marketing electronics to a mass audience, introduced the TRS (Tandy Radio Shack) 80 Model I.

Commodore, maker of hand-held calculators, took the plunge and introduced the PET.

Then the rest of the world jumped in. Entrepreneurs, corporations, shamen, geniuses, bankers, San Fernando Valley housewives, adding machine companies, photocopy companies, and, finally, IBM, all introduced personal computers or peripherals or programs to a waiting but cautious world.

*"The equivalent of 10,000 transistors
in this little thing? Amazing."*

Chapter Three
Of Programs and Programming

There is a misconception in the land. The misconception says that, in order to program your computer, you must learn something special, like programming. You don't.

To program a computer, all you need to do is put a disk in a disk drive, or put a cassette in a cassette player, and push a button. That's it. Within a short period of time (several seconds for the disk; several minutes for the cassette) your computer will be programmed.

Here is a program called The WORD. It is available on either 5¼- or 8-inch disks. The program will, within seconds, turn a personal computer into a 45,000-word spell-check dictionary.

A personal computer is like a TV. In order to watch a program on television, all you do is turn it on and set the dial. To change programs, all you do is turn the dial or, more frequently these days, push a button. If none of the programs offered by the stations appeal to you, you can program the TV yourself by playing a video tape or a video disk.

It's precisely the same with a computer. The difference is that, more often than not, you'll start by playing a tape or a disk. (In the world of personal computers one does not *play* a program, one **runs** a program. You would *run* a checkbook program or *run* a word processing program.)

Pardon me for over-making this point, but you have no idea how many people are terrified by personal computers because they've heard how much trouble it is to "program the thing." Programming the thing is as easy as programming your cassette player to play a Beethoven sonata. Running a program is as easy as playing a tape.

There is a great difference, however, between *running* a program and *writing* a program, and therein the confusion lies.

Writing a program for a computer takes a lot of work. First you must learn a computer language. Like any alien, computers have their own languages. These are the ones you may have heard bandied about in computer magazines — BASIC, Fortran, Pascal, Assembly, and so on. Although these languages are not as difficult to learn as, say, Latin, they are far more difficult than pig-Latin.

Second, computers are precise and exacting. If, in a long program of thousands and thousands of lines, there is *one* character out of place, chances are the computer will not run the program properly.

Third, since writing a computer program is, like any other writing, a creative act, one never knows quite how it's going to turn out until the product is finished. It might not, in other words, work. Or it might work in some parts but not in others. Or it might work the first five times but not the sixth. Or....the variety of ways in which a program *won't* work is infinite.

Some computer languages.

The causes of these irritating and often unpredictable program failures are many and varied, but they all fall under the general classification of **bugs**. The painstaking process of removing bugs is known as **debugging**. Trying to get all the bugs out of some programs is like trying to get all the bugs out of a picnic.

It is little wonder, then, that writing programs has a generally negative reputation among ordinary humans, rather like the reputation the Polar Bear Clubs have. I cringe when I even *think* about the news footage of those people, in bathing suits, cutting holes in the ice and jumping in. *Voluntarily.* I likewise cringe when I see a program printed in a computer magazine — page after page after page of numbers, jargon, and meaningless symbols. The thought of having to copy — much less write — all of that nonsense is enough to put a person off computers permanently. (Alas, in too many cases, I fear it already has.)

This is further complicated by the choice of words those who write programs use. Generally, they don't say, "I had such trouble writing a program last night." Instead, they say, "I had such trouble *programming my computer* last night." (Emphasis mine.) This is like a Polar Bear Club member casually mentioning that he or she "went for a swim." In February. In Vermont.

It should be pointed out that some people *like* jumping in cold water, and some people *like* writing computer programs — and some people like heated swimming pools and pre-written, pre-tested programs. I don't think you'll have much trouble guessing which category I fall into.

Writing a program for a computer is the same as making your own program for television. It can be done and it can be fun, but if you're like most people, the majority of what you watch on television was made by others, and the majority of what you run on your computer will be written by others.

There was a time — only six or seven years ago — when there were no prepackaged, commercially available computer programs. This was because there were so few personal computers. (The first one, you'll remember, was introduced in 1975.) Besides, at that time small computers were in the hands of the hobbyists, and programming the computer was *part* of the process. Back then you might just as well have asked someone to come in and do the soldering on your Heathkit as buy a prewritten computer program.

This corresponds to the early days of recorded sound. After Edison invented (almost by accident) the phonograph, the only practical use he could conceive for the device was as a dictating machine. For the first decade or so, the average library featured more homemade recordings than store-bought. "Grandma Parkins on her 80th birthday." "Uncle Seth sings 'Oh Susanna.' " "Reverend Thompson readin' from the Holy Writ."

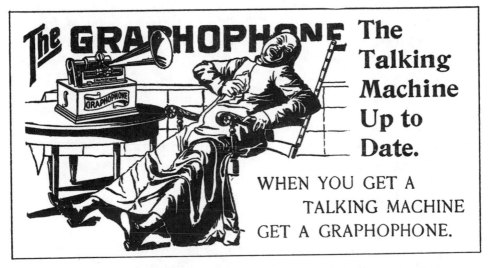

The GRAPHOPHONE

The Talking Machine Up to Date.

WHEN YOU GET A TALKING MACHINE GET A GRAPHOPHONE.

John Philip Sousa and Caruso did for the phonograph what Milton Berle and Sid Caesar did for television or Visi-Calc did for personal computers. People wanted the *program* so much that they were willing to buy whatever machine was necessary to play the program on. (The machines — phonographs, TVs, computers — are known as **hardware** and the programs — tapes, videodisks, records — are known as **software**.)

VisiCalc is a program that allows one to enter column after column of interrelated information — an electronic version of the spreadsheets businesspersons have been using for years. The difference with VisiCalc is that, when a change in one figure in one column is made, all the other figures in all the other columns change accordingly, automatically, instantly.

Now this may not mean much to ordinary folk, but to businesspeople this was a breakthrough in trade on a level with, say, opening the Suez Canal. Hours of figuring cost projections eliminated. Days of waiting for revised estimates reduced to seconds. The all-important "bottom line" was never more instantly reached, and the hundreds of components that resulted in the bottom line were never more manageable.

VisiCalc was designed to run on the Apple II Computer. The whole package — VisiCalc, Apple, and video screen — ran around $2,500. *Never mind* $2,300 of that was for the Apple and the video screen and $200 for the VisiCalc. Businesspeople wanted VisiCalc, and if they had to buy an Apple to go with it, so be it.

VisiCalc has become the best selling computer program of all time. It in no small way contributed to Apple's success. Soon, of course, every computer had its version of an electronic spreadsheet program. There are now dozens available, all lumped under the general category of VisiClones.

Another advance in the marketing of programs was **CP/M**. CP/M stands for Control Program for Microprocessors. It is a program that tells the computer how to retrieve and store information on disks. Prior to CP/M, there were several different systems for storing information — all incompatible. (Apple, Radio Shack, IBM, and Commodore still use incompatible formats.) CP/M allowed the smaller computer manufacturer to offer a machine with a standardized disk operating system. If a machine was "CP/M compatible," it could run almost any program written in the CP/M format.

With thousands of Apples (and Radio Shacks and CP/M-based computers) in the field, it became profitable for companies to market software — and so they have. Today there are thousands of prewritten programs, covering a wide range of subjects, from games to business to ecology.

We'll discuss some of these in the chapters that follow, although a full review of all available programs is far beyond the scope of this book.

There is a difference, however, between running a computer program and watching a television program. Computer programs generally require some interaction, whereas television programs will go on and on, totally oblivious to what you are or are not doing.

Learning to interact with a computer program, like learning how to use any tool, can take from one minute to several months. Computer programs are tools. They will help you get your work done with less effort and in less time. Like tools, computer programs come in varying degrees of complexity. Some tools, like the hammer, can be learned within a few minutes. Other tools — the lathe, for example — would take longer. And so it is with computer programs. Space Invaders might take two minutes to learn, an accounting program several weeks. But, like tools, once learned, they may take years to master.

Programs that are easy to learn are called **user friendly**. I'm not sure what programs that are not easy to learn are called, but I've run into a few user unfriendly ones, and a couple that have been downright hostile. One must be careful, however, that the friendliness does not become a burden after one learns the program. The training wheels on a bicycle are helpful but, if not eventually removed, may prove cumbersome.

Learning to operate a new program will require time. Even if you already know how to drive, learning the locations of the various knobs and dipsticks on a new car will take some study and patience. If you've never driven (i.e., operated a computer) before, the investment of time and patience will be greater.

Programming a computer is effortless, learning how to use that program will require some time and study, but you will never, ever — unless you really want to — have to write that program yourself.

"You know, Santa, if I had a personal computer and a modem, we could handle next year's gift list with a great deal more efficiency."

Chapter Four
Data Banks

Data banks are like money banks. Money banks gather, store, and distribute money; data banks gather, store, and distribute data.

Data are (yes, "data" is a plural, the singular being "datum," although the use of "data" as a singular is becoming more widely used) anything that goes into a computer, everything stored in a computer's memory, and anything that comes out. "Data" is a general word, like "writing," that covers a broad spectrum of information.

A personal computer can store a limited amount of data — limited in not only amount, but also timeliness. Larger computers (known as **mainframe** computers) can hold almost unlimited amounts of information, and the operators of large computers can afford to have that information constantly updated.

One could not buy a program that would give up-to-the-minute stock market information. One could not buy a program that told the ongoing happenings in, say, Pakistan. One could not buy a program that gave the current price of gold, or the temperature in Tokyo, or which market in town had the lowest price on canned orange juice.

You could, however, rent time on a larger computer that *could* tell you all that — and a great deal more.

There are companies whose business it is to maintain massive amounts of information on a vast variety of subjects, and to rent access to that information by the hour.

The three largest data bank companies are CompuServe, The Source, and The Dow Jones Information Service. CompuServe and The Source offer a potpourri of information, while The Dow Jones Information Service, as you may have guessed, specializes in business — and especially stock market — news. (The Dow Jones company publishes *The Wall Street Journal* and is the instigator of the famous Dow Jones stock market averages — "The Dow Jones Industrials are up one-half point in heavy trading.")

To use the services of one of these data banks is

relatively easy. First, you'll need a modem so that your computer can send and receive information (data) over regular telephone lines. Some personal computers require, too, that you run special "communications software" whenever you use a modem.

Then you dial the local telephone number (or the toll-free WATS number) of the service you want, and enter your identification number and password (given to you when you subscribe to the service). That's all there is to it — you are then "on line" with the world, or at least as much of the world as a given data bank is willing to offer.

Let's take a closer look at the three most popular data banks.

The Source is owned by *Reader's Digest*, "From condensing articles to expanding the limits of personal computing, *The Reader's Digest* is serving *you*."

To subscribe to The Source, one must fill out an application and pay $100. "Can't I just give you my Visa card number over the phone, and you give me an account number and a password?" I asked when I called to subscribe.

"Oh, no," the woman at the other end responded, almost shocked by the impropriety of my question. "We must have a signed form on file before you can use The Source." She articulated the words "signed form" particularly well, as though she were talking to someone who was not very good at understanding English.

A bit more than a month later my unsigned form arrived in the mail. I signed the form, returned it, and two weeks later a notebook arrived UPS.

The notebook was a standard three-ring binder with elaborately printed pages telling everything The Source had to offer — and a few things The Source did not have to offer.

It seems the *New York Times* had removed their data bank from The Source because the *New York Times* rented their data bank at more than $100 per hour and The Source was renting it for less than $25. This was fine as long as The Source specialized in those "toy" home computers but, as personal computers grew more sophisticated and widely used, the *NYT* found that more and more people were dropping the $100-plus service and getting the same information from The Source for under $25. The *Times* dropped The Source.

Dropped by The Source was a rather interesting plan called Legis-Slate that would have allowed one to track any piece of legislation through any state or federal legislative body. It sounds like an ambitious project, and it was — a bit too ambitious.

The Source still has a great deal to offer, including the news of United Press International, detailed stock market reporting, and a vast assortment of programs and information services for both home and business.

After some fiddling (data bases require that one use a **dumb terminal**, or its equivalent — and some smart computers struggle against ever becoming dumb again), I entered my ID number, then my password (if "GNLQFC" qualifies as a word), and I was "On line with The Source."

I was welcomed to The Source and urged to check the monthly discount specials offered by Comp-U-Star, The Source's at-home shopping service. I was then presented with The Entry Screen.

The entry screen gives one the choice of having an overview of The Source, instructions on how to use The Source, being shown The Source Main Menu, or going directly into the Command Level.

A menu in computing, like a menu in a restaurant, lists all that's available. The command level lets one bypass the menu and go directly into a program, rather like saying to the waiter, "Skip the menu and bring us two cheeseburgers."

The Main Menu on The Source looks something like this:

1. News and Reference Resources
2. Business/Financial Markets
3. Catalog Shopping
4. Home and Leisure
5. Education and Career
6. Mail and Communications
7. Creating and Computing
8. Source*Plus

These are the general headings under which hundreds of other choices are listed. If one were to choose "Home and Leisure," for example, the secondary menu would read:

1. Games
2. Advice & Horoscopes
3. Travel & Dining
4. Entertainment
5. Home Finance

Each of these choices would have an additional menu, and so it would go until, by a process of refinement, one would arrive at the information or program one wanted.

From the main menu I chose #6, "Mail and Communications." The Mail and Communications sub-menu was:

1. Mail
2. Chat
3. Post

Simple, direct — and I knew nothing more about The Source's "Mail and Communications" services than I did before. I pushed "1" for Mail. I was told, by yet another menu, that I could check my mail, or send mail to someone else. I love mail, so I thought I would check my mail. This being my first ten minutes on The Source, naturally, there was no mail. "You have to send a letter to get a letter," as my mother used to say. Still, I thought there might have been a welcome note from someone at The Source, something akin to the free box of chocolates you get when you check into the Ritz Carlton in Chicago.

But, no, there was no mail. Did I want to send a letter? I had my choice of anyone on The Source. The trouble was I didn't *know* anyone on The Source. For a moment I considered sending a letter to myself, but then I thought that the computer at The Source might think me pathetic, so I decided not to.

I went on to #2, "Chat." Chat allows one to have a video-to-video discussion with anyone who happens to be on-line with The Source at that time. Again, not knowing anyone on The Source severely limited my use of this feature. (I later discovered that, by using Directory, one can find out the ID numbers of everyone on-line who has an interest in, say, photography. You can also list yourself and interests in the Directory and who knows? Maybe someone will call and Chat with you.)

I moved along to #3, "Post." Post is sort of an electronic classified ad section. One can post a message in any of 75 categories, such as art, antiques, automobiles, and so on. I went right to "dating." I was told there were 27 entries. They were rather mild, compared with some "dating" classifieds I've read, but not bad considering the source of The Source is *The Reader's Digest*. "Ever made it with a programmer?" one asks. "Two women want to meet straight men in San Francisco," reads another. (Good luck.)

In addition to the general classification, each ad has a "Subject" entered by the person placing the ad. One need not read the entire ad if the subject does not appeal. (The Source's version of a plain, unmarked envelope?) One subject line was "1 YEAR OLD GIRL WANTED!" Prurient interest or no, I had to read that ad. It was, as expected, placed by a fairly young, fairly inexperienced typist. The ad itself read, "IF ANY GIRL OUT THEERE IS 14 AND LIKES GUYS PLEASE CONTACT ME."

Another young man entered the following classified at 12:07 AM: "IF YOU ARE LOOKING FOR A CHARMING 17 YEAR OLD DO NOT HESITATE TO GET IN TOUCH WITH ME." He either thought his message could stand a bit of clarification, or was it just the impatience of youth?, because at 12:16 AM he was back with another ad, "IF YOU ARE LOOKING FOR AN ATTRACTIVE 17 YEAR OLD MALE THEN GET IN TOUCH WITH ME." Androgynous charm or masculine straightforwardness, one has one's choice.

I do not mean to imply that The Source is merely a video version of a singles' bar (although they do feature extensive information on wine). No, there's Jack Anderson, too. And weather, sports, dining guides, movie reviews, commodity prices, and on and on and on.

I recommend calling The Source directly (toll free 800-336-3330) and asking for their current catalog of rates and services. If you are not happy with The Source within the first 30 days, the $100 registration fee is refundable, less charges for actual on-line time. If you are not happy with The Source any time after 30 days, you can register a public (public to all other Source subscribers) complaint on a bulletin board known as "Gripes."

The computers used at data banks have large disk drives that permit almost unlimited storage.

More liberal than The Source with their initial sign-on policy is CompuServe. All it takes is going into your local Radio Shack store and plunking down $19.95. You can't get more liberal than that. Finding a Radio Shack store that *has* the dumb terminal package (the package for computers other than Radio Shack Computers) is another matter. One Radio Shack Computer Center — in Beverly Hills no less — didn't have it. "When will you get one in?" "Oh, in two to four weeks."

I decided to let my fingers do the walking to the other Radio Shack Computer Centers, and found one that had the Dumb Terminal Package. I talked to a salesman — let's call him Ollie — and asked him to hold one dumb terminal package for me.

When I arrived at the store, Ollie was especially happy to see me. Were things that tough that the commission on a $19.95 sale would cause such friendliness? He said he was holding the dumb terminal package for me and would be right out with it.

Moments later Ollie wheeled out a box the size of a small dishwasher. "Here's your dumb terminal package," he announced proudly.

Now, I was an assistant manager of a Radio Shack store in my younger, more desperate days, and I knew that Radio Shack wouldn't sell the *box*, much less the contents of a box that large, for $19.95. What he was trying to sell me was a dumb terminal. "No, I want the package for CompuServe," I explained.

"Yes," Ollie said, still counting his commission, "This gets CompuServe. This gets Dow Jones (I am convinced he thought Dow Jones was a TV program like *Barney Miller*). This gets everything." Before he could tell me about the Radio Free Europe option, I explained that I already *had* a terminal, and all I wanted was an ID number and a password.

Another salesman, thankfully, overheard my comments. He pulled a notebook off a shelf and showed Ollie what I was looking for. There was joy as understanding dawned in Ollie's eyes, followed by disappointment as he realized his commission would not be as great as he had hoped.

While Ollie calculated the sales tax (and his commission) on $19.95, I opened the package and read a little. It was a standard Radio Shack software folder they must produce by the millions. It had a three-ring binder with two slim booklets in it, one describing CompuServe, the other describing The Dow Jones Information Service. The inside front cover had eight cassette tape pockets standing empty. (Radio Shack still markets a great many programs on cassettes.)

A sealed packet contained my ID number and password. I knew this because the packet clearly stated: "For security reasons your User Identification Number and Secret Password should be kept separate. Memorize your Secret Password, then keep it in a safe place." One's brain is not a safe place, I take it.

The packet also said, "Obtain the local network telephone number for your area at the point of purchase." Ollie asked for $21.24, so I assumed that this was my point of purchase. I showed Ollie the sentence. He read it and gave me a number. I wrote it on the packet. I apologized for the mix-up, took my change, and went home.

The basic CompuServe package includes one hour on both CompuServe and the Dow Jones Information Service. These hours must be non-prime time — after 6 PM for CompuServe and after 8 PM for Dow Jones, anytime weekends and holidays.

Somewhere around seven that evening I put my computer into the dumb terminal mode (after doing it once for The Source it was easy) and called the "local network telephone number." Ollie answered. He had given me his phone number.

"Ollie," I said, "Do you have the number for CompuServe?"

"Oh, yes," he said, and rattled off another phone number. With minor trepidation I dialed the number. Would it be his sister? Another phone in his house? A deli? New Delhi? One thing was certain: it was not going to be CompuServe. It wasn't. It was the Radio Shack Computer Center.

Not prepared for an elaborate explanation, I blurted

out, "What's CompuServe's number?" The salesperson gave me a phone number, I checked to make sure it wasn't Ollie's, and dialed it. I got the welcome, high pitched noise that means "The computer on this end of the line is ready. Turn on your modem." I did, and was on-line with Compu-Serve in a matter of minutes.

(If you have trouble getting connected with or operating The Source, they supply a toll-free number. CompuServe had no such number.)

The CompuServe main menu was:

1. Newspapers
2. Finance
3. Entertainment
4. Communications
5. CompuServe User Information
6. Special Services
7. Home Information

9. MicroNET Personal Computing

What the phantom "8" once represented is never told. Did the *New York Times* pull out of CompuServe, too? Could there have been a run on the data banks?

Although it covers the same basic territory as The Source, CompuServe appears to be a marginally lighter-weight information service. Still, it's fun, and certainly worth $19.95 for a trial hour of poking about its programs and services. (A booklet on CompuServe's offerings is available from Radio Shack, Fort Worth, Texas, 76102.)

The Dow Jones Information Service, on the other hand, is heavyweight all the way, and I mean heavy in the heaviest sense of the word. This is big time, big business, and it's very serious. No *Off The Wall Street Journal* here.

The Wall Street Journal is represented, as are *Barrons*, the *Dow Jones News Service* (known around the Big Board as the Broadtape), and transcripts of the television show *Wall Street Week*.

Also available are stock market quotations (delayed 15 minutes, as they are on all services), plus in-depth financial reports on all New York and American Stock Exchange companies and 800 selected over-the-counter companies.

The Dow Jones Information Service has a toll-free customer assistance number, but its hours do not include late-night nor Sundays. They are reachable at 800-257-5114.

"Hello. Dow Jones Information Service. Computer Room. Tim speaking. Oh, hello, Mr. President. No, there's been no sign of an upswing in the economy in the last 45 minutes. Yes, sir. We'll call you just as soon as it happens. Thank you, sir. Goodbye."

Between programs you buy and run, and data banks which you rent by the hour, the personal computer becomes a powerful tool, one that is capable of doing all the things for home, business, and education we're about to explore in Part II of this book.

"If I had a computer,

I'd com-pute in the morning,

I'd com-pute in the evening,

All over this land . . ."

"You promise me a computer and what do I get? Nothing.
Get off the cat. Nothing. That's what I get."

PART II

The Uses of
Personal Computers

"Come on up. I'll show you my Atari."

Chapter Five
An Overview of Part II

Personal computers are just that — personal. People buy — or do not buy — personal computers for the same sensible or capricious reasons that they, say, get married, or move to New York, or buy a new car.

For some people, the fact that a computer can do just one thing is enough. Young people fall in love with a specific video game with the same passion that previous generations pined away for little red wagons or model trains. If having 24-hour access to that game means owning a computer, so be it. Businesspeople might find the ability to send and receive electronic mail more than worth a personal computer's cost. The fact that a personal computer can process words ten times more efficiently than even the best electronic typewriters is all that many writers need to know.

Yet, for most people, the decision to buy or not to buy a personal computer is less clear cut. Yes, it would be *nice* to have a machine that does this and this and this, but is it worth $5,000, or $3,000, or even $99.95? And if money is not an object, then time is. Is it worth the time it will take to learn how to use this new gadget? That espresso machine from Christmas, 1979, is still sitting in the kitchen cupboard, and it has yet to make a single cup of coffee.

For most people, the decision to buy a personal computer is a process of crystallization. When a crystal is formed, say an ice crystal, the temperature of the water falls and falls, the molecules move slower and slower, yet it remains water. Then, suddenly, around 32° F — or 0° C, for you metric fans — the liquid turns to solid and a crystal is formed. The water does not become harder and harder, like drying wax, until it's eventually solid. One moment it's a liquid, the next moment it's a solid. The water has crystallized.

I have observed people, while deciding to buy or not to buy a personal computer, go through the same process. You hear about personal computers for the first time —

some mention of corruption in Silicon Valley on *Sixty Minutes* — but the water temperature remains a balmy 72°. (Since we have, as a nation, officially abandoned metric, all temperatures given will be in Fahrenheit.)

Then you hear about computer games, electronic mail, discount shopping. The water falls to a nippy 53°. Then someone actually *demonstrates* word processing, accounting, electronic spreadsheeting. The temperature dips to 39°.

Then a friend says how much fun he had "chatting" with a stranger in Oregon. Another friend said she made an airline reservation without having to be put on hold and listen to Muzak courtesy of the Friendly Skies. Yet another friend tells how he lost at chess, but he lost to a computer program that beat Bobby Fischer. The water drops to 34°, and the Polar Bear Club Members arrive en masse.

Finally your grandmother calls and says that she stayed up until 3 AM playing Ms. Pac-Man. That does it. The temperature falls to 31°. The crystal has formed. Your next major life project: Get a computer.

The next several chapters are designed to lower your water temperature. Even if you are already below the critical 32° mark, it might pay to read through this part of the book. The chapters *What Personal Computers Do Not Do Well* and *The Drawbacks of Personal Computers* may raise the ambient temperature a few degrees; and making the rounds of computer stores can be like high noon on the Sahara.

The uses of personal computers have been arbitrarily divided into several chapters, exploring the benefits of personal computers in the home, in business, in education, word processing, and games. This is an overlapping group of headings. Certainly word processing could take place in business, in the home, and in education. Games, too, could fit into the same three categories. Education — especially with personal computers — need not be limited to schools; there's lots to learn and teach in the home and in business.

Above all, please do not use this section as the definitive guide to what personal computers can and cannot do. Even as I write it, it is obsolete. Each day, dozens of new programs are introduced. Each week, several new features are offered on data banks. Each month, a new peripheral or a new personal computer expands the dimensions of personal computing.

Please view this section, then, as an introductory overview. In a few years, this part of the book will appear as silly as the middle section of the 1950 edition of *The TV Book* as it attempted to describe the 1949 television season.

As programs and data banks continue to grow, so does the appeal and usefulness of personal computers.

"Frankincense is very nice, but I was sort of hoping for an Atari."

An early tabulating computer.

Chapter Six

Personal Computers in Business

Immediately following the triumphant success of The 1890 Census Machine, the first place computers went, naturally, was business. The company Herman Hollerith, inventor of the 1890 Census Machine, joined did not eventually call itself International *Business* Machines for nothing.

The computers of the early 1900s were nothing more than tabulating machines, and there was little need for tabulation in the home. The 'rithmetic third of the three Rs was more than enough to handle domestic calculating needs.

Besides, even if uses for a computer in the home *were* found, the consumer market was glutted by far less expensive — and far more useful — inventions. The telephone, gramophone, electric light, automobile, washing machine, gas stove, and radio — not to mention indoor plumbing and central heating — were of more interest to the average householder than a faster way to count.

The **FIRST FLUSH**

Business did have a use for the computer, but it did not adopt the new machine all at once. In the first place, computers didn't do that much. One would have to have needs as specific as the U.S. Census Bureau's to require a computer. In the second place, labor was cheap. Why pay vast amounts of money for a machine to add, subtract, and count when qualified bookkeepers could be had for twenty cents an hour?

As the years went on, however, the computer's capabilities rose — as did the minimum wage — and by the time IBM joined the hallowed ranks of the Fortune 500, one would be hard pressed to not find at least *one* large computer in each of the other 499 companies.

When the personal computer arrived on the scene in the middle of the 1970s, computers were an accepted part of Big Business. The idea that a computer cost hundreds of thousands of dollars and that it had to be programmed at a cost of many thousands more, was so ingrained in the psyche of Big Business that personal computers, costing less than $5,000 — and a pre-written program costing less than $500 — were, for the most part, ignored.

But soon, inroads were made. By the late 1970s there were three types of computers: mainframe computers, costing from $20,000 on into infinity; minicomputers, costing from $5,000 to $20,000; and microcomputers, costing less than $5,000. For a while (a time span that seemed like decades but lasted only a couple of years), the formula was set: If you were a big business you bought a mainframe, if you were a small business you bought a mini, and *nobody* in business bought a micro. To buy a microcomputer for a company was like buying a manual typewriter — no one who was serious about business would even consider it.

VisiCalc, the electronic spreadsheet program mentioned in Chapter Three, changed all that. It was acceptable to buy a microcomputer — usually an Apple — because it performed a necessary financial function that no other office machine could duplicate. The only rule was that the micro be treated with the respect due any other office machine, and not with the respect due a Computer. One could speak fondly of one's Selectric or Xerox or Apple, but one must never hold one's micro in the same reverent light as one would hold The Mainframe.

As programs developed, the businesspersons found that their micros could do far more than electronic spread-sheeting and games. By the time micros stopped being called micros and started being called personal computers, a small computer was an accepted — and invaluable — part of all business, large and small. The final nod of acceptability was given when IBM — *the* IBM — introduced a personal computer of its own.

In the corridors of big business, however, personal computers are not known as personal computers. *Nothing* is personally owned at AT&T. Neither are they known as individual computers, as individuality is not stressed among the ranks of the fortunate 500. In these halls of commerce, personal computers are known as **desktop** computers. IBM is helping to change that, too, by calling their desktop computer The IBM Personal Computer. It's a confusing world, nomenclature.

———————◄══◙══►———————

The most obvious beneficiary of the personal computer is the small businessperson. Finally, the benefits (and, alas, headaches) of the computer age are available to even the smallest of small businesses.

A single personal computer can handle accounting, inventory control, word processing, financial projections, and so much more. For the past thirty years these have been the domain of the large computer in the large company, and the cause of endless paperwork in the small company. (Payroll, for a small company, is still best handled by one's bank.)

As it did in big business, a computer can save a small business large amounts of money, while simultaneously increasing productivity.

A gradually-expanding one-person company might find a personal computer would delay the hiring of a second person for some time. Word processing speeds correspondence and accounting eases billing such that a one-person company can remain a one-person company through a doubling or even a tripling of business.

A two-person company (The Boss and The Secretary) might never need to become a three-person company. The Secretary can process so much more information with a personal computer — providing he or she can pry The Boss away from stock market analysis or Missile Command — that the need to become a three-person company might be indefinitely postponed. The Boss might even want to get a personal computer for him or herself.

A three-person company (The Boss, The Secretary, and The Bookkeeper) would find one computer a help, two computers a blessing, and three computers a luxury. The Secretary could do word processing, The Bookkeeper accounting, and The Boss could keep an eye on the commodities market without disturbing the flow of either correspondence or receivables.

In the small companies noted, each personal computer will roughly double the output of The Secretary and The Bookkeeper. The Boss, due to the intrinsic nature of bossdom, could find his or her productivity increased ten fold — or may find the personal computer just an expensive toy. Given that The Boss's productivity remains the same, a personal computer could allow two persons to do the work of three, and three to do the work of five.

After three, however, one reaches a point of diminishing returns. As companies grow, it is necessary to add personnel who are not aided by the addition of a personal computer. Maintenance, messengers, envelope stuffers, warehousing, and similar physical activities are not within the domain of a personal computer's enhanced efficiency.

A salesperson would find that the primary benefit wrought by personal computers is their ability to churn out masses of personalized letters. This would no doubt increase sales, but a salesperson would still spend most of the time on the phone or on the road.

For The Secretary and for The Bookkeeper, almost without exception, the personal computer would be a Godsend.

The benefits personal computers offer The Secretary we'll discuss in the chapter *Word Processing*, and the

A Course in Practical Salesmanship
Tuition FREE~All Expenses Paid

IN these times of keen business rivalry, the services of the Trained Salesman command a high premium.

The Oliver Sales Organization is the finest body of Trained Salesmen in the world. It is composed of picked men, and is under the guidance of Sales Experts.

In less than ten years it has placed the Oliver Typewriter where it belongs—in a position of absolute leadership.

Its aggregate earnings are enormous and the individual average is high.

The scope of its activities is as wide as civilization and the greatest prizes of the commercial world are open to its membership.

The organization is drilled like an army. It affords a liberal education in actual salesmanship, and increases individual earning power many per cent, by systematic development of natural talents.

Its ranks are recruited from every walk of life. Men who had missed their calling and made dismal failures in the over-crowded professions have been developed in the Oliver School of Practical Salesmanship into phenomenal successes.

The Oliver Typewriter puts the salesman in touch with the men worth knowing—the human dynamos who furnish the brain power of the commercial world.

Because every Business Executive is interested in the very things the Oliver stands for—economy of time and money—increase in efficiency of Correspondence and Accounting Departments.

The OLIVER Typewriter
The Standard Visible Writer

is simple in principle, compactly built, durable in construction, and its touch is beautifully elastic and most responsive.

In versatility, legibility, perfect alignment, visibility, etc., it is all that could be desired in a writing machine.

It's a constant source of inspiration to the salesman, as every day develops new evidence of its wide range of usefulness.

Just as the winning personality of a human being attracts and holds friends, so does the Oliver, by its responsiveness to all demands, gain and hold an ever-widening circle of enthusiastic admirers.

If you wish to learn actual salesmanship and become a member of the Oliver Organization, send in your application **immediately,** as the ranks are rapidly being filled.

You can take up this work in spare time, or give us your entire time, just as you prefer.

Whether you earn $300 a year, or **twelve times** $300 a year, depends entirely upon **yourself.**

We offer to properly qualified applicants the opportunity to earn handsome salaries and to gain a knowledge of salesmanship that will prove of inestimable value.

Can you afford to vegetate in a poorly-paid position, when the way is open to a successful business career?

Address at once.

THE OLIVER TYPEWRITER CO., 161 Wabash Ave., Chicago

[1906]

benefits to The Boss we'll explore later in this chapter, when we look at personal computers in the executive suite. But, for now, let's see what favours personal computers offer the typical small business bookkeeper. At the same time we'll look at the fears office workers have of computers, where they come from, and how to eliminate them.

The language of accountancy is numbers. Objects the size of locomotives are reduced to model numbers and inventory figures. Everything is broken into its smallest components, and each component has a part number. Pieces of paper are referred to by check number, invoice number, and purchase order number. Each transaction has a transaction number, each service a service number, and each employee an employee number. To a bookkeeper, God is the ultimate accountant, because it is said that He has numbered even the last hair on our heads.

Computers, like bookkeepers, take particularly well to numbers. All the figuring, copying, and keeping accurate track of ciphers is what computers were created to do, and they do it magnificently. They do it so well, in fact, that the superior speed and ability computers have over humans in this area has given rise to the various boogie-man-computer-taking-over-the-world scenarios.

And it is this very fear of "taking over" that can keep a personal computer at the door of an accounting department, longing to get in. The bookkeeper may fear that, once he or she has taught this "thing" everything about the financial workings of the company, the position of bookkeeper will be replaced by a four-dollar-an-hour typist.

Nothing could be further from the truth, and if you are an employer looking to cut costs by *replacing* your bookkeeper with a personal computer, you might as well abandon that idea right now. A company needs someone — a human being someone — to keep track in a numerical way of the ebb and flow of products, materials, people, time, and, of course, money. A computer cannot do this, but a computer can *assist* a human in doing this by removing the miasma of repetitive detail that prevents the human from seeing the larger picture.

In a small company, it is important that the person operating the "accounting computer" has a firm grasp of standard accounting procedures, as well as a knowledge of how company money came and went before the computer came along. The personal computer is an efficient tool in bookkeeping, just as are pencil and paper and general ledger books and electronic calculators. Tools require humans to work them and, the more skilled the worker, the finer the end result.

Another fear many people have is the fear of the unknown, and computers, more than anything, represent "the unknown." Paper is knowable. You can touch it, feel it, write on it, read from it, stack it, file it, fold it, spindle it, mutilate it, and throw it away when you're done with it. But a magnetic disk? A piece of plastic or aluminum covered with rust? "*This* holds the equivalent of fifty general ledger pages? And *this* holds the entire customer file, complete with credit ratings and records of orders and payments for the past five years? And *this* holds the entire inventory, with cost-per-piece, supplier, and year-to-date sales for each item? I want nothing to do with it."

More mysterious is what goes on *inside* the computer, in those dark places where the sacred one-through-nine are transformed into zero-and-one; where precious digits go through the rather violent-sounding ritual of "number crunching."

Fear of computers is very real. It even has a name, cyberphobia — from the word cybernate, meaning to control or become controlled *by* (evil, evil) a computer. This fear affects, according to some estimates, as much as thirty percent of the population. Those thirty percent would never dream of reading this book, any more than people with an even more widespread fear would ever consider reading **The Spider Book.**

An illustration from "The Spider Book."

At work, however, if the boss brings in his or her pet tarantula — or his or her pet computerization project — the employee has three choices: find a new job, find a way to conquer the fear, or find a way to kill the thing. One never knows how a cyberphobic employee will respond, and it is a wise and compassionate employer who has a gradual plan for introducing personal computers into the mainstream of company life.

Here are some suggestions on easing computers into the workplace.

1. Start by dropping subtle hints. In the middle of a task that a worker finds particulaly dull and time-consuming, casually mention, "If we only had a computer, we could get this done in ten minutes." Computers can and do eliminate dozens of boring and repetitive office procedures, and the thought that one never again had to alphabetize the mailing list or add an endless column of numbers might spark some curiosity about this awful machine.

2. For every task you point out that a computer can do, point out three that it cannot. Whenever an employee performs a task that required ingenuity, intelligence, wit — or even hands — be sure to say, "We'll never replace *you* with a computer!" Be sure to stress the "you." This is known as positive reinforcement. It is important to get across the point that personal computers in small businesses do not replace people, they help people do their jobs easier, faster, and better.

"We'll never replace you with a computer."

3. Talk to people about the *idea* of getting a computer. Do not announce one day, "You're getting a computer — what kind do you want?" To some people that's like announcing, "We're moving to Afghanistan — how do you want to get there, by boat or by plane?" Start slowly with the concept, and build from there.

4. Discuss *programs* rather than *computers*. Computers are, to most people, fairly uninteresting machines. It's the *programs* that do the work, and in that lies the fascination. Point out what a spell-check program or an electronic spreadsheet program or an accounts receivable program might do and how it works.

For example, the PeachTree Software Company has Invoicing and Inventory programs that tie into their Series 8 Accounts Receivable program. These programs have speeded up the processing of invoices by several magnitudes around Prelude Press.

The customer's name and address are added only once. At that time discount percentage, credit limit, billing terms, and other information specific to that account are "keyboarded in." The customer is assigned a code name or number — "BD134" is the code we assigned to "B. Dalton

Bookseller Store #134," for example. (It's in the Puente Hills Mall, Pomona Freeway at Azusa, in beautiful City of Industry, California, for you bookstore trivia fans.)

For the purposes of this demonstration, however, let's create a mythical bookstore, The Mythical Bookstore. The customer code for The Mythical Bookstore is MYTH. Let's say The Mythical Bookstore sends in an order for five copies each of **The Personal Computer Book** and **The Word Processing Book**.

Standard accounting practices would require checking the credit rating of the store (do they have an outstanding balance due? Is it overdue? Does this order take them over their credit limit? What discount do they get?); filling out a shipping order; filling out a packing list; filling out a shipping label; figuring out the amount due; writing an invoice; recording the amount and date of invoice on the customer card; adding the amount of the sale to the daily order sheet (which will eventually be added to a periodic order sheet, which will eventually make its way to the general ledger); deducting the number of books ordered from the running inventory report (which eventually makes its way to the master inventory report); filing a copy of the invoice; and sending a copy of the invoice to The Mythical Bookstore.

With that amount of paperwork to ship ten (or two) books, it's little wonder that small publishers — like small businesses everywhere — find it, shall we say, a challenge, making ends meet.

With the PeachTree Invoice and Inventory programs, however, processing an order is quite a different matter.

To check the account's financial status, one types in "EC" for "Examine Credit." The program then asks for the customer code. We enter MYTH. In a moment, all the pertinent data concerning The Mythical Bookstore is displayed on the screen, including address, credit limit, date of last debit, amount of last debit, date of last credit, amount of last credit, year-to-date sales, year-to-date payments, and so on. (At this point, by the way, the human element comes irreplaceably into play: Should we send ten more books or should we not?)

One exits the Examine Credit mode by hitting the ESCAPE key (a key found on almost all personal computers that, as the name applies, will get you out of things). One then types "EN" for "ENter Invoices." (Yes, they do have an "ET." It's for "Enter Transactions.") Once again one is asked for the customer code. Again, we type in MYTH.

The date, which was keyboarded into the computer when it was first turned on earlier in the day, is automatically entered as the invoice date, although this date can be easily changed. (Whenever a program automatically selects something, it is known as the **default** setting. It saves adding frequently used parameters — such as dates in accounting or margins in word processing — over and over again. Defaults can generally be overridden by a simple command or two.)

The program remembers the last invoice number and assigns, as a default, the next available number. The shipping and billing address of the store are displayed, as are the discount, invoice date, terms, and so on. If all of this is acceptable, one moves to entering an invoice; if not, one can change anything on the screen.

Let's assume all the default settings and information from the customer file are accurate. To enter five copies of **The Word Processing Book**, one types the department code (which we have assigned as a dash, since we only have one department) and the product code ("WP" in the case of **The Word Processing Book**). One then enters the number of copies ordered (5) and moves onto the next title, **The Personal Computer Book**. The department is, again, " - " and the product code, in case you haven't guessed, is "PC." The number ordered, five, is entered, and the only remaining factor to add is the shipping charge. (The books are for resale, so they are not taxable.) The rest of the invoice — including all figuring — writes itself.

The entire invoice printed below was written using only the following commands: EN, MYTH, -WP, 5, -PC, 5, and 2.43.

```
Prelude Press
Box 69773
Los Angeles, California
90069
                              INVOICE NO.: 575757

                              INVOICE DATE: 11/26/82

                                  PAGE: 1


      The Mythical Bookstore              The Mythical Bookstore
SOLD  11011 Made Up Road            SHIP  11011 Made Up Road
 TO   Fabrication, Utah              TO   Fabrication, Utah
      12345                               12345


                                    CUSTOMER ID..: MYTH
  SHIP VIA.:                         P.O. NUMBER..:
  SHIP DATE: 11/26/82                P.O. DATE....: 11/26/82
  DUE DATE.: 12/26/82                OUR ORDER NO.:
  TERMS....: 0-30-30                 SALESMAN.....:


PRODUCT I.D.      DESCRIPTION     ORDERED   SHIPPED U/M UNIT PRICE   AMOUNT TX

-  WP          Word Processing Book   5.00     5.00 EA     5.37        26.85
-  PC          Pers. Computer Book    5.00     5.00 EA     5.37        26.85
FREIGHT        Shipping                                                 2.43

                                            NET AMOUNT:               56.13
                                                   TAX:                0.00 *
                                            TOTAL DUE:               56.13
```

If that weren't enough, the program also removed five copies of each title from the inventory figures, posted the debit against the store, and recorded the entire transaction in a temporary file that can later be added — automatically, of course — to the general ledger.

Similar descriptions of programs and the benefits they offer should be enough to coax all but the most critically cyberphobic into the computer age.

5. (Four was a long one, wasn't it?) Whenever possible, let the operators choose their own program. The choice of the computer itself is probably best left to The Boss for all those Boss-type reasons — cost, service, availability, do-I-

have-a-brother-in-law-in-the-computer-business — and it's a good idea to get the same make and model computer for everyone.

Fortunately, the more business-oriented personal computers do both accounting and word processing with equal ease. The peripherals for each machine might vary — accounting might require a hard disk while word processing might only need floppies, but word processing would require a letter-quality printer while accounting might only need a dot matrix — but the basic computer itself should be the same.

This allows for multiple-machine service contracts, second system discounts, employees feeling comfortable with each others's machines, the availability of at least one back-up computer during breakdowns, the ability of machines within an office to communicate more easily with each other, and so on.

The software, however, is another matter. Who knows better which accounting program will meet the company needs than The Bookkeeper? And who already knows more about the way words are processed in the office than The Secretary?

Personal computer programs that do the same things might do those things in very different ways. Personal computer programs have, yes, a personality, and that personality will have to interact with the personality of the person operating the program. It's best to let the person who will be interacting the most choose the program he or she will be interacting with.

Also, selecting an accounting or a word processing program is no easy matter, and being given the task will get a possibly reluctant employee more involved with the idea of personal computers long before the computer even arrives.

6. Give your employees time. Give them time to explore, compare, and select their programs. Give them time to read up on personal computers and their uses. Give them time to visit computer and software stores.

When I say give them time, I mean give them *paid* time. Give them one or two afternoons a week to do nothing but explore the land of computers. This might mean reading, this might mean visiting stores, this might mean lying down with a cold compress on the head. Let their readiness, their crystallization process, come in its own time — but let it come on company time.

When the computers and programs finally arrive, give them time to play with the computers, fiddle with them, learn the basics. Do not expect any output from the computer for a while. A program is a complicated — and often frustrating — thing to learn. If there is pressure from The Boss to turn out a trial balance or a mass mailing, well, you remember about the straws and the camels.

The best way to learn a program is by doing — trial and error — and in doing, some work might get accomplished, but don't rely on it. During training time, work will, in fact, be slower than usual. (Some recommend that a dual set of books — one on the computer and one on paper — be kept for at least six months *just in case*.)

7. Reward your workers for acquiring a new skill. This might mean a raise or an extended lunch hour or a bonus or however you wish to acknowledge that you have not only a Secretary and a Bookkeeper, but also two skilled Computer Operators as well.

Small computers are not just for small companies. More and more, personal computers are making their way into all levels of business, large and small.

In the executive suite, managers are finding that the financial services offered by The Dow Jones Service, CompuServe, and The Source to be invaluable. Like an answered prayer one never thought to pray, executives are peering into video screens from coast-to-coast and sighing, "How did I get along without it?"

The news, travel, stock quotations, research, shopping, and electronic mail features of the various data banks can be valuable and, every so often, a game or two might be in order.

The programs for the personal computers of

managers and executives is vast. After the success of VisiCalc, software vendors stumbled all over each other to offer not just electronic spreadsheets, but financial projection and business planning programs of all sorts and sizes.

These programs are designed to be run by the executive personally — not handed to an underling with the instructions, "Run these figures through the computer." The difference between direct contact with the program, and being one or more levels removed is remarkable. Direct contact encourages fiddling, nudging, experimenting, trial runs, and the sort of creative fooling around that sometimes results in a work of genius.

"Hands on" computer operation in the executive suite also removes the time lag between the idea and the "numbers." Figures can be figured on the spot — no two hour or two day wait while someone visits the mainframe.

Once executives become comfortable with their personal computer, they might even try a little (shhh) word processing. Few will admit to it, of course. Typing is for typists, not for bosses. However, a great many people find that their thoughts are not as clearly communicated through dictation as through the more traditional method of pen-to-paper. Most of these executives will find that writing on a personal computer is even more productive than writing by hand.

Someone once said that if correspondence is a part of your job, you are a professional writer. There are few professional writers I know who can successfully dictate. Most try it out, but return to the pen or the keyboard. It seems to work better that way. Many executives who try word processing find that they prefer it to dictation for important letters, proposals, and reports.

Most people tend to overwrite, and the speed with which one can remove the excess on a personal computer is remarkable. More about this in the chapter on word processing.

Outside the executive suite, personal computers are finding a home on other levels of big business as well. Various departments in charge of this or that find a personal computer programmed to do this or that as useful as the adding machine is to the accountant or the typewriter is to the secretary.

Cost projections, amortizations, research, airline reservations — the list is endless. Chances are, whatever a department does, there's a computer program — on disks or in a data bank — that will help do it better, faster, and easier.

Word processing is one of the things personal computers do best. Every expensive electric typewriter you see is a perfect place for a personal computer running a word processing program. The reasons for this are detailed in the next chapter on word processing, but let's consider for a moment word processing specifically in the large corporation.

Here, reprinted from **The Word Processing Book**, are six reasons why twenty personal computers with word processing programs *might* be a better buy for a large corporation than one large computer with twenty terminals.

1. It takes a long time, a lot of money, and an unbearable amount of expert consultation to decide which large computer to buy. Further, it is often difficult to justify the expense of buying a large computer for word processing alone. Higher-ups will say "Well, we already have a computer. Let's use that one." The computer in the data processing department may be ill suited for word processing, or may be too small to add a dozen extra terminals. And how do you prove it will do any good once you got the big computer? This takes yet another study, and another study takes more time and more money. And on and on and on.

Buying a personal computer or two, and having them replace a Selectric or two, is not difficult. Within six months you'll have information, from within your own company, on how they are doing. If the results are positive, then several more machines can be added. If the results are favorable six months later, you can get a word processing computer for everyone. It'll take a year, but that will be less time than most corporations spend researching and buying a large computer.

"And then we're going to put the printer over there in that building. Would you like to see?"

2. There is a fear of computers among some office workers. In starting slow, you can give word processors to those who are anxious to have them. They will use them well, the fearful will learn that there is nothing to fear, and within a brief period of time, the formerly frightened will be demanding a computer of their own.

3. How often have you heard the phrase "Our computer is down?" Like most of us, computers do "get down" from time to time. If twenty people are dependent upon one computer for all their word processing needs, you can imagine what happens when the one computer stops working. If, however, you have twenty separate computers, and one breaks, it's hardly noticed. In larger corporations, having an extra word processing computer "in reserve" would be a justifiable — if not intelligent — expense.

Why couldn't they offer the choice, "experienced and clean?"

4. Since a word processing computer is nothing more than a personal computer programmed for word processing, it is very easy to run other programs and have the computer do almost anything else. One executive, for example, might need to have accurate stock market quotations. Another executive might find financial projections using one of the many electronic spreadsheet programs invaluable. A third might need ongoing airline information, a fourth might use electronic mail, and so on.

Rather than a terminal attached to an inflexible large computer, you have the advantage of many small computers and the flexibility they offer.

5. If it happens all at once, the transition from individual typewriters to one large computer can be a nightmare. The addition of individual word processors can take place gradually, over a period of time, and the overall workflow of the office need not be disturbed.

6. Twenty personal computers, complete with printers and word processing software would, at $7,000 per computer, cost $140,000. You can *easily* spend that much money researching, purchasing, and programming a large 20 terminal computer.

There are situations in which it is far more economical to buy one large computer. I mention the advantages of individual word processing computers because, if you call in a word processing expert who has spent the last ten years installing nothing but large-scale word processing operations, it is doubtful that he or she will mention any of the above. It is, in fact, possible that he or she might not even *know* any of the above. Personal computers have been around for very few years. Many of the Big Computer experts continue to look upon them as toys.

But toys they are not. Personal computers are tools, and it's been a long time since a tool as varied, versatile, and infinitely useful to the business community has come along.

Chapter Seven

Word Processing

Having written an entire *book* on word processing, I want this chapter to be complete. I wish there were a way to print the entire contents of **The Word Processing Book** here, complete with Dore etchings and turn-of-the-century typewriter ads, but that would make this book twice as thick (and twice as expensive).

Maybe I could reproduce it in miniature, like the twenty volumes of the *Oxford English Dictionary* reduced to two volumes and a magnifying glass. But then the magnifying glass would make this book thick and expensive, too.

In addition, I suppose there are some people who don't want to hear as much as I have to say about word processing. Some people just want a nice, simple overview so they can go on to the chapter on games. So, here's a nice, simple overview, and for those who want to know more about word processing, well, I can recommend a great book on the subject.

Computers, as we have discussed, are good at processing numbers. Numbers go in one end, get sorted and resorted (processed), and come out the other.

Computers are good, too, at processing words. They do this, as you may have guessed, by turning words into numbers. To be more accurate, computers turn *letters* into numbers.

To symbolize all of the letters, numbers, and punctuation marks of the English language, we would only have to assign, say, one hundred binary numbers. (26 upper-case letters, 26 lower-case letters, the numbers 0 through 9, and 38-or-so punctuation marks.)

The accumulated literary output of humankind — from **The Bible** to Dante to *The National Enquirer* — could be written using only the symbols 0 and 1.

(A computer could process a language with a more intricate set of characters — such as Chinese or Japanese — by simply assigning a different binary number to each character. The problem, of course, is getting all those char-

acters on a *keyboard*. In Japan, one of the most techno-
logically advanced nations on earth, the majority of business
correspondence is still done by hand.)

While using a personal computer to process words,
you would never know that your deathless prose was being
reduced to a succession of 1s and 0s. You type on the
computer's keyboard — which is like the keyboard on any
typewriter — and words appear on the video screen.

Since the words on a video screen are written with
electrons on phosphor, and not with ink on paper,
changing the words is easy. This ability to effortlessly
change whatever has been written is central to computerized word processing's power and popularity.

The processing of words, however, does not take place
in a computer. Word processing takes place in the human
mind. The computer is simply a tool to help recall what
has already been written. If you look at the sentence, "To
be or not to be; that really is the question," and decide to
remove the word "really," that processing of words took
place not on paper or on a computer screen, but in the
mind.

Writing is like sculpture. Michelangelo once said
that he saw a form within the marble, and all he did was
remove everything that was not the form. And so it is with
writing. From the words in one's vocabulary, one selects a
clump of them that best fits the idea at hand. Then, by a
gradual process — known as polishing in sculpture and
editing in writing — the excess is removed and the final
work stands alone. This process is as true of writing a
letter as it is of writing a sonnet.

Once one sees how easy the removal of the unwanted
verbiage is, it becomes easier to get the words out of the
mind and into a concrete form. Many people think that
writing must flow from the mind preedited and perfected.
The inability to meet this impossible task is a major cause
of writer's block, abandoned novels, and unanswered correspondence.

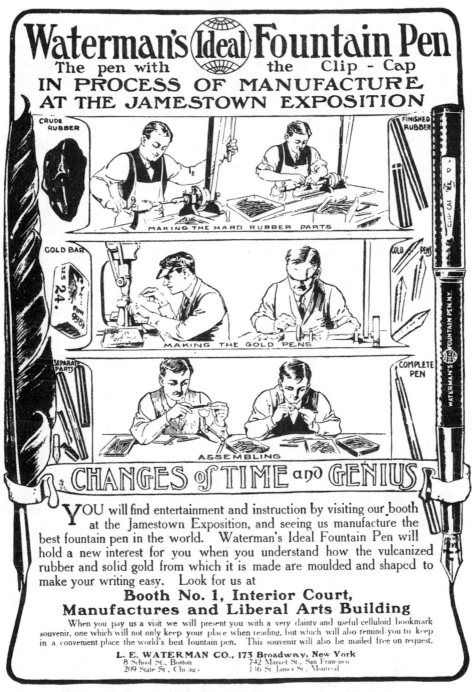

How an inexpensive word processor is manufactured.

A personal computer offers a midway point between the finality of ink on paper and the capriciousness of thought in the mind. On a video screen, the words are there, but because they are so easily changed, it's almost as though the "bad" ones (the ones that will eventually end up *not* there) don't count. At the same time, the "good" words (the ones the Almighty intended to be there all along) are preserved. Once *all* these words are down, separating the wheat from the tares becomes a comparatively easy task.

After perfection has been reached, the personal computer's printer will type one copy or one thousand copies at speeds sometimes faster than 500 words per minute.

In addition to flexibility, personal computers offer speed.

For example, take a program known as The WORD Plus. (It used to be called "The WORD," then they improved it and it became "The WORD Plus." When they improve it again, I have no idea what they'll call it — "The WORD III?" "The WORD Plus Plus?" "The WORD Plus Some More?" Time will tell.)

First you run a word processing program and write something with it — a letter, a novel, a poem. Then you run The WORD Plus. It will, for example, count the number of words you have written. It took The WORD Plus less than six seconds to tell me that there are 1,672 words in this chapter.

Giving it another command, The WORD Plus took another five seconds to tell me that this chapter had 534 unique words. (By using 534 words, I repeated some of them and came up with a 1,672-word chapter.) Then The WORD Plus checked each and every one of those 534 words against a 45,000-word dictionary, and printed a list of all the words that did not match (indicating possible misspellings and typos). The WORD Plus did this task, which would have taken me — at the rate of two words per minute — almost five hours, in 47 seconds.

The WORD Plus will look up a misspelled word and give several alternate (correct) spellings. If the misspelled word were "thier," The WORD Plus would recommend "their," "thief," and "tier." This looking-up takes five seconds. It takes me more than five seconds to find my dictionary, much less a word in it. After the user selects the correct word from the list (as bad as I am at spelling, I know the word I'm looking for is "their"), The WORD Plus *replaces* the incorrect word with the correct word in the text. There were 23 incorrect words in this chapter. The WORD Plus replaced all 23 of them with their acceptable-to-Mr.-Webster spellings in less than 40 seconds.

These examples of speed are not just indicative of The WORD Plus (although it is a remarkably fast program). It is simply an example of the speed with which personal computers operate when doing specific, repetitive tasks.

Most word processing programs have a feature known in Computerese as **global search**. Global search will find anything within a document in a matter of seconds. (In word processing, whatever you happen to be working on is known as a **document**, a **file**, or **text**.)

If you wanted to return to the point in a long document in which you were writing about Pittsburgh, all you'd do is ask the word processing program to find "Pittsburgh." Before you could spell Pennsylvania, the program would deliver you to Pittsburgh. If that wasn't the specific mention of Pittsburgh you were looking for, with a simple command global search would take you to the next occurrence, and so on.

Most word processing programs can find something, then replace it with something else. This is known as **global search and replace**. Margaret Mitchell's publisher would have found global search and replace delightful. The original name for the heroine of **Gone With the Wind** was Pansy O'Hara. Just before going to press, Ms. Mitchell changed the name to Scarlett.

An improvement, I'm sure we all agree. Can you imagine Clark Gable passionately clutching Vivien Leigh while Atlanta burns and saying, "I love you, Pansy." But can you also imagine the work some lowly copy editor at Macmillan must have had finding every occurrence of "Pansy" and changing it to "Scarlett?" Might as well try changing the word "sin" to "mistake" each time it appears in **The Bible**.

With global search and replace, one would ask the word processing program to find "Pansy" and replace it with "Scarlett." This process could either be automatic, or the replacement could take place selectively, the operator being asked by the program each time, "Shall we replace this one?" The latter avoids unintentional replacement, and would eliminate such sentences as, "Scarletts bloom in the spring, and Aunt Pitty Pat wore some nestled in her hair."

The search and replace function comes in handy while doing form letters. A letter written to Larry could become personalized to Mary within a few seconds. Each would have a personally typed letter — personally typed by your personal computer, that is.

Some programs allow you to merge an entire mailing list into a form letter, automatically replacing name, address, and any other information that changed from letter to letter. The computer would turn out page after page after page of individually typed letters.

Different word processing programs offer different features. One of my favorites, available on almost all programs, is known as **word wrap.** When the end of a line is reached while typing, word wrap automatically puts the next word on the next line. No more hitting the carriage return button, except at the end of paragraphs, while writing poetry, or making lists.

Word processing programs that turn personal computers into word processors cost from $50 to $500. If you write two letters a month and send out Christmas cards once a year, you'll find the investment in a less-expensive word processing program worthwhile. If you are a writer — as a profession or an avocation — a more sophisticated word processing program is more than a worthwhile investment — it will change your life.

> Computers are becoming more familiar and easier to use. Businesses are no longer necessarily dependnt on large cneral sysms; individutteals wihin organizations no longer necessionels to interpret their needs in language which the computer can understand.
> —*London Times.*

Chapter Eight

Personal Computers in Education

Because personal computers are infinitely patient, they make excellent tutors.

Because almost everyone under thirty living in this country was raised with — and perhaps on — television, most young people feel more comfortable looking at a video screen than being with another human.

Because personal computers are interactive, a student may get more individual attention per day from a computer than per month in a classroom.

These reasons, and many more, make personal computers an inevitable part of education's future. For the present, however, the average school teacher need not fear being replaced.

Personal computers do not teach, *programs* teach, and programs — like textbooks or film strips or video tapes — must be written, created, and compiled by people. There will be effective programs and there will be ineffective programs, but for the moment there are not enough of either to make a major impact on education as we know it.

Not that there's not plenty of things to learn today from personal computer programs — everything from multiplication tables to spelling to grammar to touch typing. The point is that the vast potential personal computers offer in the area of education has not even been approached, much less tapped.

The first problem is one of time. Personal computers have been around but seven years, and personal computers as we know them less than four. If you can imagine how much time it has taken to develop the variety of teaching materials available today, you'll see why four years could not begin to duplicate, much less surpass, the non-computerized educational aids.

The second problem is one of disk storage space. Even a large-capacity floppy disk with 340K of memory will hold only 170 pages of double-spaced typewritten material. I use the word "only" because — although 170 pages would be generous for, say, word processing — in education, 170 pages might not even hold a complete outline, much less all the information detailed by that outline.

The storage problem should be solved in the next few years as video disks (the kind that have so dramatically failed to capture the imagination of the home video market) are adapted for personal computer use.

One video disk could hold the entire *Encyclopedia Britannica*, including color photographs. One could theoretically store, in the same space currently occupied by an average teenager's record collection, all the information necessary for a four-year college education. Not only would that information be there, like books in a library, but the information could be cross-referenced in an elaborate system of indexes and files.

To give an example of how this might work, let's look at a program available today called Superfile. After information is entered into the computer, one "files" that information on disks under a series of key words. Each bit of information — anything from an address to a thousand-page book — can be filed under as many as 250 key words. What one can do, in essence, is file one piece of information simultaneously in 250 different files.

A letter need not be filed under either "Sales" or "Product Information," it can be filed under both — plus 248 other classifications. The names in an address book need not be filed under last name alone — first name, birth date, city, state, favorite color, astrological sign, and 243 other vital bits of information could be entered as key words.

Not only can you call up a given file from any of the key words, you can also combine key words. Only those files having all of the required key words would be displayed. Using the address book as an example, one could ask for all Capricorns from Wisconsin whose favorite color is pink.

Applying this program that already exists to the larger data bases available to personal computers in the future, we can see the value this would have in education.

The works of Aristotle need not be filed just under "Aristotle." Each sentence could be filed under dozens of different classifications, from "Ancient Greece" to "Philosophers" to the subject matter of the sentence.

"Neither a borrower nor a lender be" might be filed under Shakespeare, *Hamlet*, Polonius, Elizabethan England, England, Drama, Plays, Literature, Thrift, Borrowing, Lending, and Fatherly Advice — just for openers.

If a student were to type in "LENDING and PLAYS," all references to lending in all plays would be presented. "LENDING, PLAYS, and SHAKESPEARE" would give all references to lending in the plays of Shakespeare. "LENDING and HAMLET" would give all references to lending within the play *Hamlet*. And so on. The variations are as infinite as the imagination and curiosity of the student.

The third problem (I bet you thought there were only two) is that the market for educational software has not been as great as for, say, business programs or games. In this supply & demand economy, the supply meets the demand, and the demand for educational software has not been overwhelming. Interest in educational software has been steadily increasing, but it's not a Demand quite yet. It is now at the level of Second Request.

There are still too few computers in classrooms to spend the money necessary to develop elaborate educational software. There is a plan to give tax breaks to computer companies who donate computers to schools. The plan limits the donation to one computer per school. One computer per school is about as useful as one Selectric per typing class. But it's a start.

Most educators who want good software must write their own. Most software houses who want to sell educational programs must rely on concerned parents for sales rather than progressive school boards.

Although educational programs do not begin to approach — either in quality or quantity — what they will be ten years from now, a personal computer's other abilities could benefit almost any student today. Word processing for homework and reports; data banks for research and current events; programming for science projects; games for mind-body coordination (and fun); the list goes on.

The most valuable computer-assisted education a parent can offer a child today is how to be comfortable with computers. These television-typewriters will be around for some time. Their numbers will be increasing yearly. By the beginning of the next century (less than twenty years away), the computer will be almost as common as the television in the home or the typewriter in the office.

Familiarity with computers is generally known as computer literacy. Computer literacy doesn't require speaking a computer language, nor does it require programming skills, nor does it even require extensive knowledge of already-written programs. All it requires is a sense of ease around computers, and the knowledge that personal computers are powerful tools, not menacing characters out of science fiction.

DAILY — VARIETY — DAILY

VOL. 196 No. 53   24 Pages   Hollywood, California-90028, Thursday, August 19, 1982   Newspaper Second Class P.O. Entry   50 Cents

WILL ATARI + 'E.T.' = MAGIC?

MCA-U Sells Videogame Rights To
Blockbuster Hit For Undisclosed Sum

New York, Aug. 18 — MCA-Universal has sold the videogame rights for its blockbuster, "E.T. — The ExtraTerrestrial," to Warner Communication's Atari for an undisclosed sum. Atari has plans to have a videogame version of the feature out by Christmas.

"E.T." director Steven Spielberg is directly involved in the designing of the game. "The game will center around getting 'E.T.' home," said Spielberg. "It's going to be a challenging game, and also perhaps the first emotionally oriented videogame ever turned out. I'm very excited about joining futures with Atari," he said.

Atari was similarly excited about "joining futures" with Spielberg. Corporate spokesmen felt they might have a game which would prove to be as big as "Pac Man." "E.T.'s" image has grown so large that it is no longer just a feature but has become a product category, Atari feels, and they strongly hope that an "E.T."-based vidgame will have all the cash-pulling characteristics of its feature film parent.

As for the ability of the new game to help pull WCI's stock out of its recent slide, Wall Street observers had doubts. "It's just one of many games," said analyst Harold Vogel of Merrill Lynch, Pierce, Fenner & Smith. "I don't think you can trade the stock based on one cartridge just as you wouldn't trade the stock based on one movie."

Vogel isn't certain that the success of a feature can be used to predict the success of a videogame based upon it. He feels that past experience, where films have done well and their spinoffs have not, show the shaky basis for making such predictions.

Wall Street seemed to agree, as WCI's stock dropped sharply over the course of the day.

MCA-Universal wasn't making any comments about the sale, and about why the high-potential rights hadn't gone to MCA's own fledgling videogame effort.

Chapter Nine
Games People Play

Computer games. Is there a living, breathing human in this country who has not heard of Pac-Man? Only Johnny Carson has a higher recognition factor than this hungry circle with a pie-shaped mouth. (Pac-Man, by the way, is a Japanese invention. It comes from the Japanese word *paku-paku*, meaning to open your mouth and shove food in.)

Not since the smile button (a distant cousin of the Pac-Man), have a few simple lines, drawable by any first-grader, grossed so much money. In fact, Pac-Man, a game, has outgrossed even *Star Wars*, one of the most successful movies of all time. George Lucas, creator of *Star Wars*, reading the handwriting on the video screen, has joined with Atari, the marketers of Pac-Man, to create video games. So has Steven Spielberg, the creator of the *other* top-grossing movie of all time, *E.T.* (See article.)

The young do not need a chapter detailing the endless fascination computer games offer. Do you think the younger generation is unmotivated? Do you think they have no interests, no direction, no passions in life? Drop by the local computer-game arcade some time. You will see riveted attention, focused concentration, and rock-steady reflexes that would spark the envy of a concert violinist.

And, if you want an education in video games, bring along a roll of quarters. The Masters will be happy to teach you, as long as your quarters hold out.

Like Ping-Pong or tennis, video games look easier from the sidelines. Before you sigh that these kids are wasting their time, try a few sets. You'll see that the co-ordination and split-second timing required to play — and acquired *by* playing — these games, is nothing short of spectacular.

The Army, realizing this, have made the aiming mechanisms on their newest multi-million dollar tanks the same as the ones found on the most popular computer games. The generation that grew up with Missile Command can go to war with . . . Missile Command.

No, the young don't need to know about the wonders of video games. It's us old folks who read *books* about computers and wonder what all the fuss is about who need chapters on the wonders of computerized game playing. (The young figure that, for the price of this book, they could play Donkey Kong — or Konkey Dong, or whatever that game is — thirty-two times.)

So, I will turn the balance of this chapter over to Mr. Michael Evans, who will describe what video games are like for us non-enthusiastic — but none-the-less open-minded — non-teenagers.

Me and My Computer
A Classic Love/Hate Relationship

by Michael Evans

Recently I bought an Apple II — a friendly, attractive little home computer. Along with it, I purchased a series of programs that some humorist chose to call "games." If you detect a hint of bitterness in my remark, you're close: in short, I was not ready for the "fun and challenge" of computer games.

It all began one fine Saturday when I sat down to while away some time in computerized amusement. The game disk was labeled Penny Arcade. It contained various pinball, tennis, Ping-Pong, and lemonade-stand games, all of which looked harmless enough to the untrained observer, so I loaded it and selected a game called Little Brick Out.

Little Brick Out consists of a paddle, a ball, and several rows of multicolored bricks. On command, the computer will toss you the ball, and you must keep it from getting past the paddle. If you hit it, it will bounce off, strike a brick, and make that particular brick disappear. Each brick that vanishes adds a few points to your score, and the object is to get rid of all the bricks. Sounds easy, right? Try it sometime.

The first thing you will notice is that the screen is very bright, which makes it hard to distinguish between the multicolored bricks and the brightly colored spots that don't go away when you close your eyes. In addition, every time the ball hits an object it makes a little "bip" that sounds like a malfunctioning smoke alarm. While you are distracted, the computer lobs the remainder of the balls past your paddle, leaving you with something resembling a baseball score.

Perhaps the most disconcerting aspect of Little Brick Out is the sound it makes when it sneaks a ball past you. The buzzer makes you feel not unlike a hockey goalie who has lost the rest of his team and must face the enemy alone.

Abandoning Little Brick Out, I moved on to Star Trek, a game that evokes both excitement and a sense of personal failure.

You play the part of Captain Kirk and are responsible for the utter elimination of all Klingons from the universe. All of them. By yourself. I don't mean to complain, but somehow the odds just don't seem fair. There are 40 of them and one of you. You have a time limit: they have all day. You try to behave like a gentleman: they shoot at you while you're trying to open communications. You have to refuel and get more weapons every so often: they are somehow able to wander through space without expending any energy whatsoever. As if all this weren't enough, you can chase a slippery little Klingon clear across the Galaxy only to discover that he has borrowed a "cloaking device" from the Romulans (arch-enemies for years) and while he can still shoot at you and break vital parts of your life-support systems, you can't even see him! Why couldn't the Romulans give *us* the cloaking device? Why do the Klingons get all the breaks?

I decided to "beam out" of Star Trek and try my hand at something a little closer to home — Blackjack. First of all, the computer said that *we* cut the cards and I lost. Wait a minute. At no time did I even *see* a deck of cards, electronic or otherwise.

Before long, a message appeared on the screen saying "I'm shuffling now!" Again I had nothing to go on but the computer's word, which may or may not have had any basis in truth. Finally, it dealt the cards. It dealt both of mine face up and one of its face up and one face down. At this point, I was convinced I was being taken for a ride. Here it was, displaying my cards for all the world (and itself) to see, while I was denied the same access. And if that wasn't enough, it wanted me to bet money on the game! I tried to bet a nickel, but it came back with a message informing me that the house minimum was $5. I wondered why it felt entitled to set the house minimum in my house, but since I had gone this far, I figured it was worth $5 to continue. I typed in "5" and hit the Return key.

I had a Queen and a Six. Sixteen points. The borderline. The computer had a King showing, but no amount of persuasion would get it to let me peek at the other card. I figured it had probably "dealt" itself 21 points, so I asked for another card. It gave me a 10. Needless to say, I busted. And my opponent had 13 points, but it won anyway. (I never paid, though. I don't think it would have paid me if I won.)

I decided to try another selection. Then another. And another.

At this point, I began to wonder about the effects of computer games on my overall health. Aside from the fact that every minute spent playing games is a minute not spent playing tennis or otherwise toning my body, I began trying to guess exactly how much radiation the human body absorbs when it spends five hours a day in front of a television screen trying to destroy little space creatures with a laser turret. And why would I continue to play with a machine that obviously had the utter degradation of my sense of well-being as its primary goal?

I have a theory. I call it the Cycle of Unrequited Punishment. It goes like this. Suppose I *do* shut the thing off and turn to some other wholesome activity. How does the computer respond? Does it feel rejected and unwanted, or drop into a funk? Does it promise never to be unsportsmanlike if only I'll turn it on again?

No. It sits there, smug in the knowledge that I'm not playing with it because I know I can't win. *The machine simply refuses to recognize that it's being punished.*

Smashing it won't do any good. Its brains are etched onto silicon and encased in plastic. They, and every other part, are replaceable. And the repaired unit won't acknowledge that it's been properly rebuked. *So who's punishing whom?*

Now we've reached the critical stage in the cycle. Faced with all of this unrequited punishment, the weary computer owner tends to grasp at one last hope: the way to put that machine in its place is to beat it at its own game.

That's when the cycle starts all over. . . .

Don't get the idea that you can't win. Of course you can. The computer knows that even laboratory rats need occational positive reinforcement. Let me describe my first victory.

I decided to select a game that left nothing to chance — no dice, no cards — something based on sheer mental manipulation. Knowing better than to play chess with a machine that understands Bobby Fischer's psyche better than his own mother, I chose to play Othello, a checker-like game that requires some crafty thinking.

It began well. One of the first things the program did was ask me if I would give it an advantage. I resisted the temptation to become snide: "What's the matter, afraid you'll lose?" Instead, I just laughed and said "NO."

It set up the board and the game began. We both played well, but before long it fell for one of my traps and let me capture one of the coveted corner squares. I pushed mercilessly, taking men and replacing them with my own. I felt an almost inhuman glee. When the last chip was played, the machine beeped once to signal the end of the game, and printed.

ME: 25   YOU: 39
WANT TO PLAY AGAIN?

That was it. No fanfare, no congratulations. I beat the computer, fair and square, and all I got was a printout of the score and a question whose tone implied that my victory was of no consequence. I bitterly typed in "NO," and unplugged the machine.

In retrospect, perhaps the computer was just being game — a willing combatant. Or maybe it'll take a whole string of defeats for the computer to begin showing signs of desperation. I might even have to bring home another game disk — and win those, too — just to drive the point home.

But right now, my computer sits on the bottom of my closet. I've got to have time to think.

Thank you, Michael.

While Michael's thinking, let's take a look at a few new video games from INTELATARIVISION — "Games as Original as their Name."

Here we have ten from INTELATARIVISION'S new series, "Life is a Video Game."

THE TROJAN WOMEN

You are a male in a culture in which 98% of all top governmental and military positions are held by women. Your goal: Get an amendment giving equal rights to men added to the Constitution while raising two children.

SHOOT THE SHEEP

You are a farmer who tries to protect his sheep from
a deranged stranger. Little do you know that the stranger
is playing a video game in which he is trying to shoot as
many sheep as he can before being stopped by a deranged
farmer. Fun for all.

SCHOOL DAYS

You are a school teacher in the days before computerized education. Good luck!

THE YOUNG AND THE REST OF US

You play one-half of a young couple who have an uncontrollable passion for each other in Victorian England. Many surprises.

DIVORCE

You are pitted against Elizabeth Taylor in a race through the divorce courts. The first person to divorce and remarry the same spouse three times wins.

RIDERS OF THE LOST ARK

You are Indiana Smith, a mild-mannered professor nine months of the year, but your summer vacation is spent rounding up stolen art treasures on your flying horse, Pegasus.

I'LL SHOW YOU MINE IF
YOU'LL SHOW ME YOURS

An introduction to anatomy, presented in a way that's
sure to hold the interest of the 13-year old in all of us.

GURU YOU

You are a midget in the circus who must impersonate a 12-year old Perfect Master when the 12-year old Perfect Master is stepped on by an elephant. Your life is always in danger, but there's lots of good food and sex.

CURIOSITY

You are one of several curious monkeys, and you are put into a series of interesting situations. Educational as well as fun.

WHAT THE HELL'S GOING ON HERE?

You are shown a picture on the video screen. You have thirty seconds to offer a plausible explanation.

(The Grand National Playoffs of this game are held every year in Washington, D.C. Winners are frequently offered high-level positions in the White House Press Corps, the State Department, and the CIA.)

Chapter Ten
What Personal Computers Do Not Do Well

There are some things computers do better than people and some things people do better than computers. I know admitting that humans can do some things better than computers in a book about computers borders on heresy, not unlike praising Liberal Humanists at a Moral Majority rally. Alas, it is true: Human beings are not yet obsolete.

Some predict that the office of the future will have no need for the printed word, just one large desktop-size video screen, simultaneously displaying dozens of "sheets." This 2001 concept is known, in fact, as The Paperless Office. Some are saying this is inevitable.

I'm not so sure. Let's look at an essential element of anyone's business or social life, the engagement calendar, and see if the time-tested datebook & pencil has been superseded yet by magnetic media and computer.

To make this important comparison I purchased a "Schedule Program" ($19.95) for my computer and *The 1983 New Yorker Diary* ($13.50) for my pencil. I will not name the manufacturer of the Schedule Program as almost all inexpensive datebook programs operate in roughly the same way. We will not be looking so much at an individual program as we will be investigating the entire range of not-too-expensive electronic appointment calendars available today.

The New Yorker Diary is an 8 x 10 hardcovered volume, available in brown or blue artificial imitation leatherette. When opened, each double-page spread covers seven days of appointments. There are 23 lines for appointments (or, as *The New Yorker* prefers, "engagements") each week day, ten lines for Saturday and twelve for Sunday. (I suppose Sundays in New York are more active than Saturdays.) At the top of each page is the month and year. At the top of each column is the day and date. The lines in each column have no specific time allotted to them, except a line toward the middle of each day that is labeled LUNCH.

The New Yorker is, of course, famous for its cartoons. So respected are the creators of these often hilarious drawings that the magazine refers to them as Artists and lists them in the table of contents of each *New Yorker* along with its Authors.

These cartoons are generously spread throughout *The New Yorker Diary*, and often refer to particular holidays during the year: The wife of a Colonially-dressed couple saying to her husband, "Good Heavens! Tomorrow is George Washington's birthday and we don't have a thing for him!" or a middle aged man, kneeling by his bed as Father's Day approaches, reminding God, "I don't ask for much, but what I get should be of very good quality."

The Schedule Program comes on a brown circle of plastic, enclosed in a black square of cardboard. It also comes with eight pages of Operating Instructions. There are no cartoons on either the disk or the instructions. There is, in fact, no humor in this program at all. It could safely be used by an undertaker to schedule funerals without offending anyone.

The Schedule Program limits the number of appointments to ten per day, good enough for most Saturdays in New York, but this limitation immediately renders the program useless for doctors, lawyers, and other professional people who generally see more than ten people per working day. Further, the Schedule Program does not remind you to have lunch.

When you want to make an appointment with *The New Yorker Diary* you flip to the appropriate week, find the correct day, jot down the time and information — from one word to 23 lines' worth — and the appointment is set.

When you want to make an appointment with the Schedule Program, the first question it will ask is the year. Now I know it's 1983 and you know it's 1983, and *The 1983 New Yorker Diary* knows it's 1983, but your computer doesn't know it's 1983 any more than your toaster does. (Your computer may have a clock/calendar, in which case it would know what year it is. If this is the case, please apologize to your computer for me.) On the Schedule Program, the year is simplified. One does not have to type in "1983" each time, but merely "83." This may not seem like much, but can you imagine typing "83" when adding-to, taking-from, or checking-on every single appointment all year long?

The next question the Schedule Program asks is the date. That seems simple and straightforward enough, but I could not tell you the date "a week from Thursday" for the life of me. I'm not entirely sure what *today's* date is. To find "a week from Thursday" in *The New Yorker Diary*, all I'd need do is turn the page. I would locate Thursday, and the date would be conveniently attached.

Unfortunately, there is no "flipping through pages" on a computer. "A week from Thursday" means nothing to the Schedule Program (for reasons we'll discuss later). It wants a date, and the date must be written in a very specific way. First the month, as a number, then the date, with a zero preceding the date if it is less than 10.

This requires knowing what month it is in numbers. I'm lucky if I know what month it is in *words*. What number is April? July? It's a good thing I know November is 11 and December is 12, because I run out of fingers the end of October. Adding zeros before dates is equally confusing: I was born on the 5th, not 05. August 5th would be entered "805." September 28th, "928." November 26th, "1126." Christmas would fall on 1225, and New Years Day 101.

The Schedule Program then asks for an "Event Name," a phrase light years removed from the sophisticated "Engagements" one makes in *The New Yorker Diary*. The Operating Instructions tell us that an Event Name, like an engraved charm bracelet ordered by mail, can be "up to thirty characters in length." "Dinner with Joe" is acceptable. "Dinner with Joe at The Ravenswood" is not. Complicated addresses or simple directions are out. There is no writing-small-so-it-will-fit on a computer.

Then we are asked by the Schedule Program the time of the event. The time is to be added in hours and minutes, but without colons. 115 is 1:15, 1045 is 10:45, and 1225 is not Christmas Day but 12:25. After entering this, it will ask AM OR PM? Unless you mark "P" for PM, the program assumes AM.

Here the Operating Instructions for the Schedule Program state, "At this point you have completed one entry." Whew.

To delete an engagement in *The New Yorker Diary*, one simply turns to the page on which the engagement was written, finds the engagement, and erases it. To delete an event in the Schedule Program, one must enter the year, the date, and then the number of the event to be deleted. (The events are numbered by Schedule Program automatically from 1 through 10 according to criteria having nothing to do with Bo Derek.)

To find an available engagement time in *The New Yorker Diary*, one need only open the page, scan the week and, if full, turn the page to review the week that follows. When an agreeable hour is found, one writes the information down.

To find an open event space in the Schedule Program, one must first ask the computer to display information between two dates. This means entering the current date, an arbitrary date at some point in the future, and then scanning the scheduled events between those two dates two days at a time. (To have a full week displayed all at once would require a print-out.) When a suitable event slot is found, however, one cannot simply enter the information. One must exit the scan mode and enter the enter mode, starting with year, date, event name, etc. etc.

To use a computer as a datebook, based upon the above description, seems cumbersome — and it is. Keep in mind, though, that in the descriptions given thus far we have assumed that the computer was up and running and the Schedule Program already loaded. If the computer were turned off, or busy doing something else or — heaven forbid — broken, you can see how much more inconvenient iron oxide might be than processed wood pulp.

The fact is, simple list making and information retrieval is much more efficiently performed with pen, paper, and human interaction. As lists become longer, computers become useful for manipulating information on those lists, especially in terms of selecting specific items or rearranging items in complex patterns. The longer the lists and the more complex the rearrangements, the more helpful computers become.

Let's create an imaginary situation in which computerized scheduling might be helpful. Suppose that there were six people who needed to meet with each other on frequent but irregular intervals. When they were not meeting with each other, they have numerous meetings and activities away from this inner circle. As any secretary knows, scheduling a time in which six busy people can mutually gather is not easy. One (usually the Boss) sets a time and the others, as best they can, rearrange their schedules.

If all six, however, were to schedule all their activities on computers, and each schedule were programmed to interact with each other's schedule, any one of the six could ask the computer for blocks of time in which all six had nothing else scheduled. With a push of a few buttons, a meeting between the six could be added to everyone's schedule, and no one would have to rearrange anything. Granted, a program like this would cost much more than $19.95 but, to the participants, it would be worth it.

Airline reservation computers work in this way, but on a much larger scale. An airline agent can sell a specific seat for a specific flight, and instantaneously all connected reservation terminals the world over would indicate that that seat was sold.

Given this kind of convenience, it would be worth the inconvenience of learning to translate human expressions into "computer talk." As pointed out earlier, "A week from Thursday at four" means absolutely nothing to a computer, and programming a computer to take that simple sentence, and other similar sentences, and translate them into year-date-time would be difficult and require large amounts of memory. Is "four" a time or a place? If it's a time, is it 4:00 AM or 4:00 PM?

The sentence: "Meet June for Brunch at Fridays on Thursday around 2nd or 3rd between ten and eleven." is understandable to most people living in New York. June is the person we're meeting, Fridays is a place, Thursday is the day, "around 2nd or 3rd" is the general location, "between ten and eleven" is the time, and because brunch was mentioned we assume it to be in the morning.

Words change their meanings based upon their use within a sentence, and computers have no way of knowing which definition of what word to use when. This is why the high hopes scientists had for using computers to translate foreign languages have been substantially lowered in recent years. When a computer tried to translate "The spirit is willing, but the flesh is weak" into Russian, it came out "The vodka is good, but the meat is rotten."

The computer wouldn't know what to make of the brunch sentence. You would no doubt get an appointment on June 2nd or 3rd between ten and eleven, if you were lucky to get anything at all. And is that ten or eleven AM or PM? Is it for Thursday or several Fridays in a row? And who is this Brunch fellow?

For most of us, I think, although we may love our personal computers dearly and use them for everything from writing love letters to alphabetizing our record collection, there will still be $13.50 set aside toward the end of December for the following year's *New Yorker Diary*.

"If God had meant man to have a computer, he wouldn't have given him a brain. That's what I say."

Another example of pencil & paper being better suited than computer & program is checkbook balancing. To enter a check in a checkbook you write in the check number, the date, who the check was written to, the amount of the check, and subtract that amount from the bank balance. Most people don't even do the last bit of subtraction. Some people don't do it for years. Some people never do.

Can you imagine these people turning on a computer, putting a disk in the computer, entering the date (Month/Day/Year), entering the check number, entering the payee, deciding what the check was for, is it tax deductible? is it a household expense? a business expense? medical? legal? social? and answering all the other questions a prying program might ask.

Sure, for the first few weeks such a program is fun. You might even look forward to writing checks and watching the computer magically tell you how much money you have in the bank — something you could have done with a $5 pocket calculator. After a while, though, the thrill wears off, and if you aren't organized about your finances now, you will not be organized about your finances six months after The Electronic Solution arrives.

Computers will accurately record, add, and subtract a row of checking deposits and debits, but doing it "the old fashioned way" is faster, easier, and cheaper.

Keeping an electronic checkbook is valuable for large businesses who need to know exactly how much was spent in which of several dozen departments. This uses the sorting feature of computers, and sorting is a thing computers do very well.

But humans are not bad at sorting, either. If you really need to know how much you spent last month for food or auto or medical expenses, sorting the checks into little piles when the monthly statement comes from the bank wouldn't take more than fifteen minutes.

Naturally, at tax time, it might be good to know how much was spent on deductible items and how much on non-deductible items. Again, sorting the year's checks into three piles, "deductible," "not deductible," and "hopefully deductible," would take no more than an hour. Besides, most people fill out the short form and take standard deductions anyway.

Speaking of taxes, many people seem to think that a personal computer will somehow file their taxes for them. Well . . .

Tax laws change from year to year. During Reaganomics, they change from month to month and, when Congress is in session, sometimes from day to day. Given the lag time in marketing computer software (six months at least), even if you were to buy an up-to-date tax return program, it might not be as up-to-date as you might hope.

Most of the tax return programs I have seen are in the $100 range. Most of the come-as-you-are-and-bring-your-shoebox-full-of-receipts-and-cancelled-checks-and-W2-forms-and-we'll-turn-them-into-a-tax-return-guaranteed-to-give-you-a-refund-and-keep-you-out-of-jail-or-my-name-isn't-Henry-Block tax services seem to cost less than that. Further, I would think that these tax services would be more current on tax laws, and more experienced in personal tax returns than even your personal computer.

Another area people talk about the personal computer revolutionizing the world is in the kitchen. Trade in your file box full of recipes for a computer programmed with recipes. Well . . .

In terms of filing recipes and displaying recipes, the file box with 3 x 5 cards will do just as well as a computer and cost, oh, $2,000 less.

The place a computer might come in handy in the kitchen is reducing or increasing recipes. Enter a recipe for four and have the computer increase it to six, or reduce it to one. If someone does *a lot* of that, a computer might be a handy tool.

For everyday use, however, if two cups of flour are required to make turnovers for eight, one cup will be required to make turnovers for four, and performing such difficult calculations in your head will save you not only some dough, but also dough on your keyboard, your video screen, and your disk drives.

I do not mean with this chapter to throw excessive amounts of hot water on your delicate crystallization process. I am, obviously, all for personal computers. I think, however, that being "for" something includes being honest about the limitations inherent in that something. I am all for compact cars, but not when moving furniture.

It's better, I think, to have your expectations lowered to a more realistic level now, than be disappointed later. If you try something that personal computers do not do well, and discover that personal computers do not do that well, you may never try some of the things that personal computers *do* do well, thinking that that, too, was nothing more than zealous hype. And that would be a loss.

Chapter Eleven

Personal Computers in the Home

The American home is such a wonderfully varied place.

There are the mama-papa-kiddie households of the Norman Rockwell paintings. There are bachelor pads. There are eight stewardesses sharing two-bedroom apartments in four different cities with timetables and work schedules more intricately planned than a space shuttle launch. There are crash pads. There are senior citizens "living together" because, if they got married, one or the other might lose his or her Social Security. Teenagers in their first apartment. Widows and widowers living alone, or with their children, or with their parents. Divorced singles. Unmarried parents. Recluses. Communes. Farms. Cities. Small towns. Big towns. Apartments. Co-ops. Frame houses with white picket fences.

I am not for one moment going to pretend that there's a "typical" American home, any more than I'm going to explore how a personal computer would "fit right in."

A personal computer either will fit right in, or it won't fit right in, and that will depend upon the needs, the interests, the curiosities, and the budget of the people in each home. It's in the home, more than anywhere else, that the "personal" aspects of the personal computers can be seen.

The programs for personal computers in the home are not as vast or directly useful as, say, the programs for business. As time goes on, this will change. Just as TV programming expanded and improved as television reached more and more households, so too will computer programs become more interesting and sophisticated in the years ahead.

The household that buys a personal computer today is still on the pioneering edge of this much-touted computer age. Estimates are that from one-to-two percent of all American homes have a personal computer. That's not a high percentage. There are more Cuisinarts out there than computers.

While some find it fun being a pioneer, others find it unsettling being even a settler. They will wait until there are towns and Holiday Inns and indoor plumbing. And, sooner or later, computerdom will have all that. Sooner or later is not yet here.

Most households, I think, buy a personal computers for the games, just as most businesses once bought personal computers for VisiCalc. Once in the home, however, they experiment with a few of the other things personal computers can do — maybe a little word processing, maybe a little data bank dating — and expand, in that household, the horizons of personal computing.

A disk drive added here, a modem there, a printer, more programs — and soon one could almost run a small business. Add a few business programs and you can remove the "almost" from that last sentence. Osmond Family and Smith Brothers: watch out!

Personal computers encourage not just children, but the child in all of us — that bubbling mass of curiosity and love of adventure — to explore not only the outer world, but also the inner world of our own potential.

Think you have a story worth telling? A poem worth writing? An idea worth expressing? Get a word processing program and tell it, write it, express it. With some computer programs you can even set it to music.

Think you could write a better program than the one you just paid $29.95 for? Give it a try. Fortunes have been made sitting up late at night, peering into a flickering screen.

Feeling artistically inclined? You might try your hand at computer graphics.

Want to know what's going on in Philadelphia tonight? Find out who's "on line" at The Source or CompuServe from that city and "chat" with them. There are no strangers in the world of personal computers — a lot of strange people, but no genuine strangers. There are certain advantages to frontier life, and the friendliness of fellow pioneers is one of them.

Or you could have your biorhythms charted, your I-Ching thrown, or your astrology read.

And don't forget the games. Games have been a central part of hearth and home for centuries. Getting together over a game of Snafu or Adventure or Star Trek can be as rewarding as gathering together to play Monopoly or Parcheesi or Mahjong.

To discuss the typical uses of a computer in the home is as hopeless as trying to define the typical home. But for those of us who take on the hopeless tasks of the world, and take them on in our homes no less, let's hope they continue to write programs to help us on our way.

Chapter Twelve

Computers and Kids

Kids *love* computers. Not only do computers embody something kids are completely familiar with, the television screen, but computers *respond*. *The Smurfs* don't respond. *Captain Kangaroo* doesn't respond. Even *The Electric Company* doesn't respond.

Computers respond.

It's funny: To an entire generation, computers represented the very personification of distance, aloofness, unfeeling, and uncaring. To the current generation (no pun intended), computers are friendly, cuddly, personal, and fun. How quickly things change.

Kids don't seem to mind learning a new language, if that's what it takes to talk with their new friend. To children, a keyboard is a new avenue of communication, not the appendage of some lowly office machine.

Not only can computers respond, but they can be *programmed* to respond in certain ways. Kids thus take to programming — not because they have a business to run or a deadline to meet or a letter to write — but for the best reason of all: it's fun.

Computers hold an additional fascination to young people for an almost irresistible reason: Grown-ups, for the most part, don't know what the hell is going on. To adults, computers are the things that remind them that payments are past due. Computers are neither interesting nor fun. They are, in fact, intimidating.

Like a boy showing his mother a snake, or a girl turning a cartwheel in front of her father who can barely cart it into the house, kids delight in feeling affection for things their parents find impossible.

In the past, music has been the battleground of this war of tastes. The John Philip Sousa generation couldn't understand the younger generation's fascination for George Gershwin. The Gershwin generation couldn't comprehend the young Frank Sinatra. The Sinatra generation didn't know what to make of rock and roll. The rock generation thinks punk is going a bit too far.

But, somehow, it's the parents who bought the phonographs and who bought the records, even if they couldn't "understand a word of it." And so it is with computers.

In the delightful piece that follows, Carolyn Benson Cohen details not only the enthusiasm of youth, but also the befuddlement of parents, when it comes time for a family to confront one of the burning questions of the eighties: "Should we get our kid a computer?"

The Kid, the Computer, and Me

by Carolyn Benson Cohen

Computers represented the wave of the future,
and who wants their kid to be late for the future?

Let me begin with a parent's true confession: all my kid knows about computers was learned in the gutter. We didn't discuss such things at home. When my boy began to get curious, he had to go to the streets for answers to his questions. It wasn't that we didn't care; we just didn't know a darn thing!

The first indication I had that his tastes were maturing was when he asked for a $20 subscription to a computer magazine. It was a big jump from the five bucks we'd doled out from time to time for the cheery periodicals of childhood.

"You're only 12 years old—what do you want that magazine for?"

"I like to read it, Mom."

"Read it? Are you crazy? It's all full of numbers and symbols...." Then I remembered the little notebooks he'd been leaving around the apartment lately, little notebooks filled with—you guessed it—numbers and symbols. I turned the pages of the magazine, one eye on my blue-jeaned, T-shirted, dirty-sneakered son, one eye on the fat, glossy publication. It boasted a lot of words, as well as those mysterious numbers and symbols, and a few of the words made sense to me. I was very much in favor of his reading words. And his birthday was coming up. "O.K., but you're going to have to explain this one to your father."

The very next day the boy started asking if the magazine had come yet. When it finally arrived, they both disappeared until dinner. The evening was spent on the phone mumbling unintelligible numbers and words to unnamed friends.

We had further indication that his interests were expanding when he began to drop hints about his computer savvy. This was a child who usually kept us starved for information about his life, so, while trying to ignore his egotism, we perked up our ears. In fact, as parents sometimes do, we tried to take advantage of his conversational mood to serve our own needs:

"That's good. How are you doing in history?"

With great aplomb he vaulted over more sensitive areas and kept to his topic: "You should have seen the program Kenny and I made up after school today!"

"Kenny who?" When he was younger we knew all his friends.

"Oh, I don't know. He's one of the kids."

Computer Science, with the aid of three PETS (small computers, not dogs and cats) and a terminal hooked up to the computer of a nearby university, was taught in the seventh and eighth grades of our son's private school. He was a sixth grader but, I gathered, he spent his leisure time hanging over the shoulders of those more qualified to use the equipment. Such was the beginning of his computer experience: "Over against the wall, kid. I'm an authorized user!"

Soon he was disappearing after school to the homes of several of those boys, particularly to that of one known only as "Adams." Phoning the assorted numbers he left on the kitchen table, I discovered a network of adolescent computer junkies all over the city. My kid was hanging around with some of the local high-tech addicts.

One of the boys had a mother who taught at the school and after a P.T.A. meeting I cornered her with some questions. She bragged that she had just bought an Apple II Plus for her family. I was astounded—we had reached a whole new plateau in keeping up with the Joneses! She told me about the clever and unusual programs her darlings were writing and offered advice about what to buy when the time was right. "Your son should have at least 16 K," she warned, and for the first time I learned that my child had needs that could be measured in Ks. Ks of what, I had no idea.

For several months my husband and I mulled and mused. Could we justify such an expense? And yet, from all we had been told by the school and by our son himself, he clearly had ability. Computers represented the wave of the future. Who wants their kid to be late for the future?

Meanwhile, somebody's mother was teaching my child FORTRAN. He had gotten wind of the faint possibility that we might buy a computer and had jumped into the fray with no subtlety whatsoever. He talked about it all day. Every night before he went to sleep he lay in bed like an angel, whispering another reason why we should have a home computer. We kissed him good night and tiptoed away as he quoted memory capacities and lists of available software.

To make a long story short, we reviewed the bank account, reappraised the budget, rethought the issue, and relented.

Now, imagine that you have $1,000 or more and are going to spend it on your child. You talk to all the experts, confer, make a decision, and inform the boy of your beneficence, right? Wrong. In our case, what we knew about buying a computer could fit into a salt shaker. My husband's business associates were either blank when it came to home computers or suggested something simple "so the kid can play games." So where did we go for advice on how to spend this large sum of money? To our son. His largest purchase to date had been a $40 electronic kit on which he spent an entire summer's earnings and with which he got a much-needed "A" on a science project.

The responsibility didn't faze him. For several weeks he phoned and visited the pubescent underground of computer junkies, debated the respective qualities of the Commodore PET, the TRS-80 Model III, the Apple II Plus, and other machines with curious names and numbers, and stopped in to see his buddies at Radio Shack (where he had become well known by programming their demo). Finally the Apple emerged triumphant, and we ordered it from a company in California.

One day, not long afterward, the kid was home with a cold. He lay limply across the sofa, the huskiness of his unpredictable voice exaggerated and thickened with congestion. With a television set propped at his feet he was a docile patient, although I found his lethargy disconcerting.

When the doorbell rang I rushed to answer, thinking my son was fast asleep. There was the United Parcel Service delivery man holding a big box labeled Apple. I wondered why my parents were sending apples instead of oranges from Florida and then the truth dawned. "Mom," I said to myself, "you're going to see a real show."

I called softly to the boy, who drew himself up from some inane rerun. "Come here a minute."

When he saw the box his lassitude fell away like the afghan he had been clutching about his neck. He began to leap about like someone on a pogo stick. "It's the Apple! It's the Apple!" his poor voice cracked and bellowed. The UPS man stood with his mouth open looking at the two of us. When the pogo stick settled down to earth, he helped us tear open the box.

"Save the instructions!" I shouted as the boy triumphantly lifted out the carefully packed pieces. But he knew what everything was. I was the dangerous one, almost discarding an extra 32 K bytes of uninstalled memory we had ordered. Spotting something that looked like a row of staples, I thought it was part of the packing. "Mom! Don't!" the kid screamed, just in time.

We quickly moved some furniture and I set up a card table for the Apple, leaving the boy to figure it all out. Frankly, I was on the retreat to a room where I knew how everything worked. When school was out, he placed an emergency call to Kenny.

"Who's Kenny?"

"He's a kid who has an Apple. He knows how to install extra memory."

Across town faster than a speeding bullet, Kenny banged on the door. "Mom, this is Kenny Adams," my boy said. A swarthy child with a Kellogg smile stood poised on the threshold.

"You mean, this is Kenny *and* Adams? I thought they were two separate persons!"

Kenny walked in with an air of authority befitting his superior knowledge. He grabbed the Apple from its perch on the card table and trotted with it under his arm to the kitchen. "Gotta have a room with no rugs," he explained, as I rushed to move things out of the way. With a flick of Kenny's wrist, the top sprang off the Apple and we all peered inside. It was practically empty! On the bottom I saw a shallow layer of what looked like black Lego blocks. Kenny stuck his head, hands, and the extra Ks inside the computer, and soon declared that all was well.

The day the Apple arrived, the parade of boys began. Soon I had met all the unknown kids whose computers my son had visited. Most had first and last names by now. Some came bearing extra disk drives, some with games programs, some just to test, play, and program the latest Apple. They were nice children, of various ages and even more various sizes. They didn't ask for food, but if it was offered, they cleaned me out. They were clever and funny and polite, and thoroughly wrapped up in the world of computers. I've felt much better about the gutter and my guttersnipe ever since!

As for me, I sat down at the computer with the manual one day when the kid was in school. "Push the switch into an upward position," I read. "You will be rewarded by the 'POWER' light at the bottom of the keyboard coming on." I pushed the switch. The 'POWER' light came on. A smile spread over my face.

FATHER CHRISTMAS—"UP-TO-DATE."

Illustration by John Tenniel. From *Punch*, Dec 26, 1896.

(Slightly updated by our artist.)

"No more of my sweet favors until the computer you promised me arrives."

PART III

Selecting and Purchasing a Personal Computer

Chapter Thirteen

The Drawbacks of Personal Computers

Yes, there are drawbacks to personal computers, and I'll tell you what they are. You won't have to hear it first from Geraldo Rivera on a *20/20* expose.

There are drawbacks to everything, of course, and drawbacks must be weighed in proportion to benefits. Further, most drawbacks can be reduced or eliminated if approached creatively. So, in this chapter, we will be looking not only at problems, but also at solutions.

Here they are then, the several drawbacks (and suggested remedies) to personal computers I have encountered.

1. Computers are expensive. Personal computers cost a lot in terms of both time and money. Some people I know have enough money, but they don't have much time. Some people I know have enough time, but don't have much money. Most people I know have neither enough time nor enough money. Personal computers require a sizeable investment of both.

Will this investment pay off? Will it be worth it? Like installing a swimming pool, it's hard to know until you take the plunge. Health clubs could not exist without the remarkably high drop-out rate of their members. Fully 80% of the people who join, signing up for several years at several hundred dollars, never go near the place after the first month. If everyone who joined made use of the facilities, health clubs would be five times more crowded than they are now, a burden they would be unable to bear.

A personal computer is something that you will buy, use a few times, and then abandon, a monument to your impulsiveness and lack of determination — like a Cuisinart. Or, you will buy a personal computer, wonder how you ever got along without it, and use it daily for a variety of tasks you would never dream of doing again by hand, a living example of your good taste and practical nature — like a Cuisinart.

Recommending that you "start small" doesn't help

much. As those who bought a discounted version of a Cuisinart will tell you, most of the knock-offs were no bargain — they butchered meat rather than sliced it, and mangled vegetables rather than chopped them. The very people who might have been happy with a *genuine* Cuisinart, found the imitator unacceptable, assumed the praise heaped upon food processors was grossly overstated, and returned to the processing of food by more traditional methods.

If you want, for example, to do word processing, and attempt it on a $300 machine, you might find it unsatisfactory; whereas, if you were to attempt it on an $1,800 machine, you might be thrilled; and if you were to try word processing on a $5,000 machine, you might find yourself unable to write even a shopping list without it.

If you don't process words (or do bookkeeping, or have a passion for electronic games, or one of the other things that personal computers do remarkably well), it's hard to know if the many things that personal computers do marginally well will appeal to you enough to cause a change in habit.

If you are in the habit of calling your broker or waiting for the daily newspaper to see how the stock market is going, you might not find the allure of an updated-only-fifteen-minutes-ago stock price worth turning on your computer. In some areas, personal computers might offer more power than you'll ever need — and in other areas, they may offer much less.

I wish I could give the rather pat advice, "Try before you buy." Unfortunately, personal computing is rather like flying a plane or visiting Europe or sailing a boat — you'll never know if *you* will like it unless you try it, and trying it is expensive.

If you're uncertain, continue your investigation. If any of the "drawbacks" in this chapter seem like sound, logical, clear-headed arguments for not buying a personal computer, then you probably shouldn't get one — yet. If these drawbacks seem like intolerable nit-picking that no reasonable person would consider for more than a few moments at most, then you're ready.

How long that readiness will last is anybody's guess, and if you guess wrong, it could be a costly error.

You can minimize the chances of disappointment by lowering your expectations. Personal computers do many things well, many things not-so-well, and a broad spectrum of things somewhere between "well" and "not-so-well."

Don't expect a personal computer to change your life, unless you are a professional writer who already knows how to use a typewriter; a small businessperson who has fairly standard small business needs (word processing, accounts receivable, accounts payable, etc.); or someone who devotes a large portion of their time doing something personal computers do well (electronic spreadsheeting, stock marketing, cross-index filing, and the like).

If you don't fall into one of those three categories, it might be best if you lower your expectations to a workable minimum. By "workable minimum" I mean, don't lower them so much that you don't get the computer, but lower them enough so that disappointment will not be one of your peripherals.

Be realistic. Don't expect too much from your computer.

Another way to help insure that you'll use your personal computer more often than your Norman Rockwell Thanksgiving Turkey Platter is to choose carefully. As much as possible, select the computer and programs that meet your current needs and fit comfortably into your lifestyle.

If you want to play computer games, buy the best game-playing computer you can afford — and make sure you like the games that are available for it.

If you are running a small business, there is no need to buy a computer and software designed for a ten-million dollar corporation. (Yes, the salesperson might say, you can grow into it. When you're grossing ten million, however, you can *buy* into it.) If you get more program than you need, you'll have to learn about the complexities of a program that you might use only 25% of, and those complexities besides being expensive — might one day cause the computer to be turned off for good.

If you're just curious about computers and want to get your feet wet, a fish pond will do — there's no need to install an Olympic-sized pool.

As pointed out before, however, if you need word processing, plan on spending enough for a decent personal computer, a letter quality printer, and the best word processing program you can find. The same is true of business: buying too much computer can be a bother; buying too little, disastrous.

There's a quote about suiting the action to the word and the word to the action, but we've already quoted once from *Hamlet* in this book, and one profound Shakespearean reference per computer book is sufficient, I think.

2. Computers are powerful and, therefore, capable of powerful mistakes. It is hard to duplicate, using ordinary methods, the efficiency and effectiveness of a computer. It is equally hard to duplicate, using ordinary methods, the degree of devastation and disaster possible on a computer — unless you consider fire, flood, and nuclear fission "ordinary methods."

Let's assume, for example, that you run a company and have all of your accounting information on a single hard disk. A hard disk is a platter of metal, usually aluminum, spinning at something like 1,800 revolutions per minute, which is equal to 30 revolutions per second. Pretty fast. Let's say that one day, the hard disk decided it was tired of being a hard disk and wanted to become a frisbee.

The disk exercises a remarkable amount of free will for a disk, releases itself from its normally secure housing, and flies out the window, landing in the *Guiness Book of World Records* for The Greatest Distance Traveled by a Personal Computer Hard Disk.

Television news crews are dispatched to interview your disk, while Tom Brokaw and Roger Mudd argue over which one of them will handle the story. (Neither one wants to, but they hear that Dan Rather is opening his broadcast with it, so they feel *somebody* has to interview the damn thing, Tom Snyder and Rona Barrett having both refused.) Roone Arledge can't decide if the story should be on *The ABC Evening News* or *ABC Wide World of Sports*. He decides both.

The MacNeil Lehrer Report cancels its planned sattelite interview with Fidel Castro and devotes a special, expanded 90-minute version of the show to your disk.

Also at PBS, both William F. Buckley, Jr. and Dick Cavett are trying to get the disk on their respective shows. "The disk is a celebrity, not a politician," says Cavett. "It belongs on my show."

"The disk is a projectile, and therefore belongs on *Firing Line*," counters Buckley.

In a ceremony on the White House Lawn, your former hard disk is made an honorary frisbee. "This is one small step for disk," the hard disk says as you flip off your TV and mutter something about ungrateful hardware. You try to figure out a way to recover months of priceless financial data, and decide there is no way.

A company once, in a less colorful way, lost all of its accounts receivable information. The company sent out polite form letters asking how much money, if any, each customer owed. Not surprisingly, the company was soon out of business.

Businessman, upon being informed that his hard disk had been turned into a frisbee.

Even a single floppy disk, holding 170 pages of information, can be a tragic loss. The entire text of this book fits comfortably on three 5¼-inch floppy disks. If I were to lose one of these prior to the publication of the book, and I had failed to make back-up copies (which I almost always fail to do), it would surely go beyond tragedy and deep into soap opera. O, the gnashing of teeth and the pulling of hair. Cecil B. DeMille never directed *angst* on a grander scale than I would emote.

There are two possible causes for such unthinkable, but possible, occurrences: computer error and operator error. As much as I hate to admit it, the latter far exceeds the former. By "computer error," I mean both hardware and software. Once again, the latter is the cause of far more difficulty than the former.

The causes of costly mistakes, in order, are:

A. Operator error.
B. Software error.
C. Computer error.

Using software that's been around for a while and a computer that's a relative newcomer, the last two categories might trade places. Almost without a doubt, though, operator error will be responsible for more "computer errors" than anything else.

Suggestions for minimizing this drawback are:

First, make sure you know what you're doing. It's fine to experiment with a computer — there is almost nothing you can do from the keyboard of a personal computer that will cause any permanent damage to the machine — but don't experiment while you're working on something important or irreplaceable.

Before trying anything new, try a test first, or *at least* save whatever is in memory on a diskette. If, for any reason, the computer "crashes," (shuts down, freezes up, or turns off), whatever was in the memory is lost. If it is put on a disk (a simple, swift procedure), then the chance of retrieving the information is greatly enhanced.

Second, buy quality, time-tested software. This may not always be possible. You may need a program that is one-of-a-kind and newly introduced. In that case, watch for bugs and be very careful. If you are using the program to process information that is important to you, call the software manufacturer periodically and ask if any bugs have been reported that you should be aware of.

On the whole, however, most of the major categories

of software — word processing, spell-checking, accounting, electronic spreadsheeting, filing — have products in each category that have been around at least a year, have sold thousands of copies, and have had most of the bugs removed.

Third, take good care of your machine. It doesn't require much. It is estimated that the majority of electronic parts that do not fail within the first twelve months will last for 500 years. How they make such calculations — the transistor being less than thirty years old and the silicon chip less than twenty — I shall never know.

It's a comfort, though, to think that, unless Life Extension Science takes the same dramatic leaps as Computer Science, and soon, our personal computers will be giving pleasure to generations yet unborn. Well, maybe it won't last *that* long, but a computer should hold up until you buy your next computer.

The only parts of the computer that need periodic servicing and attention are the moving parts, and then only the disk drive and the printer. (A good keyboard seems to go on forever, and a joystick, well, use it for twenty years and buy a new one.)

Disk drives should be cleaned periodically. It takes about two minutes: all you do is put a special head-cleaning disk in the drive and turn on the computer. Most "read/write" (disk) errors are caused by dirty heads, which two minutes of cleaning would have prevented.

Even if the computer misbehaves totally and eats a disk, the failure of the operator to make a back-up disk — again, about a two-minute procedure — can cause the problem to be much larger than necessary.

Power failures, too, cause the computer to lose its memory. Power failures happen with varying degrees of frequency in various locales. While living in Detroit, I don't recall any, except during electrical storms. In New York there were only two, although they lasted several days each. In Los Angeles, the power company named in honor of Mr. Edison seems to fail, on the average, once every other month.

Murphy's Law #253A states, "The power will fail

only when you are about to find out 'whodunit' in a television mystery, have a souffle in the electric oven, or put something irreplaceable into the memory of your computer and have been too lazy to save it on a disk." Law #253B reads, "This will only happen when you are dangerously behind schedule, exhausted, and in a bad mood."

A good slogan to adopt while working with a computer is that of the compulsive bargain shopper: "Save, save, save." I am very bad at this sort of thing, but I do make it a habit to save whatever I am working on whenever I get up. Given that I get up at least every fifteen minutes, it's a rather good plan. Other people less antsy than I might want to save at the end of every page, or every ten minutes (set a timer), or at some predetermined interval or place in their work.

3. Eyestrain. Some people find that peering into a video screen causes eyestrain, and some do not. For those who do, here are some suggestions.

First, try using a monochrome video display rather than color. The images on color screens are not as sharp as images on monochrome screens. The fuzziness might be causing the problem.

Second, a monitor (a video display that plugs directly into the computer, rather than a recycled TV set) gives a sharper image.

Again, fuzziness may be the problem. (When a screen display is fuzzy, the eyes strain to sharpen the focus. This constant straining can cause headaches.)

Third, green phosphor is supposed to be easier on the eyes than white. Try a green phosphor screen for a while.

Fourth, the glare of room lights off the glass of the video screen can cause eyestrain. Get a filter (Polaroid makes a good one) that reduces the reflected light. (The Polaroid filter also improves the contrast of the characters on the video screen, making them easier to read and further reducing eyestrain.)

Fifth, try a "slow phosphor" video display. The image on a video screen changes thirty times per second. This rapid changing is what gives the illusion of motion when

Laverne hits Shirley in the face with a pie or a pizza or something. Ordinary video screens are designed to display the one-thirtieth-of-a-second-image, and then to fade quickly to make way for the next flash.

Slow phosphor holds the image for a longer period of time. Before the last image fades, another has already taken its place, and before that one fades, another has taken its place, and so on. This delivers a video display that is rock-steady.

The disadvantage of slow phosphor is that, because it holds onto a light image so long, when you change something on the screen, "ghosts" of what were formerly there will momentarily remain. These poltergeists remain for less than a second, but for someone used to quick-fade phosphor, it can be annoying. It is, however, far less annoying than eyestrain.

Sixth, read the solutions to disadvantages 4 and 5 below.

Eyestrain does not affect the vast majority of people who use video screens. These suggestions were offered for those who do have trouble.

4. Neck and back strain. Most back and neck strain experienced in front of a personal computer comes from maintaining the same posture, hour after hour.

If the keyboard and video display are all in one piece, your options for shifting positions are limited. You must reach the keys which, attached as they are to the screen, are not easily moved. This makes varying your position difficult. Not surprisingly, this sameness of position is a pain in the neck, a pain in the back, and a pain in any other portion of your anatomy you care to name.

The solution is a simple one: a detachable keyboard. A detachable keyboard allows you to place the video screen where it's most comfortable for viewing, and the keyboard where it's most comfortable for typing.

We have grown accustomed to looking *down* at a page when we type. This is because those of us who learned typing on a typewriter found that, invariably, that's where the paper was. The paper was where the typing was, and that's what we wanted to see.

Video screens can be placed a bit higher — closer to eye-level — and not having to look down for hours at a time can, in terms of neck and back strain, make quite a difference.

Also, the video screen need not be as close as the keyboard. As I write this, the video screen is at least four feet away. To read the entire screen, I only have to move my *eyes*, not my head. (The closer I get to the screen, the more my head would have to move — some law of physics at work there, no doubt.) This causes less strain on my neck and back. Further, the field of my vision encompassed by the video screen is small compared to the amount that would be involved if I were up close. I don't know if it's true or not, but my mother always told me it was bad for my eyes to sit too near the TV screen.

I will, mom's advice notwithstanding, move closer to the video screen when I edit this piece. I will be looking at the text in a critical character-by-character way. Now I'm just looking at words, sentences, and ideas. For those, four feet is close enough.

But even when I move up close, I will never be as close as I would have to be if the keyboard were permanently glued to some spot directly under the video screen.

A detachable keyboard also allows for an infinite variety of positions. Some of this chapter I have written with the keyboard on my desk, some of it with the keyboard on my lap. Were I so inclined, I could have stood up, lied down, or assumed any of a dozen other positions.

Maybe it's true that the straight-backed rigid posture is the best for long-term typing, but I never learned to sit like that, and I doubt if I ever will. There is too much else to learn before and after getting a computer. Who wants to have to worry about learning a new way to *sit?*

I would rather have a computer that adapts its shape to my posture, not one that demands I adapt my posture to its shape, especially when that shape is dictated by an 1874 invention. Personal computers with attached keyboards were modeled after computer terminals, and computer terminals were modeled after typewriters. This was because computer terminals were designed for secretaries who were already fámiliar with typewriters.

Besides, if there's any validity to the next point, the further away the video screen, the better I feel.

5. Radiation. *All* TV screens, including the one in your bedroom and the one in your living room, give off radiation. The electron gun shoots electrons, "radiating" the phosphor until it glows. Some of this radiation leaks out.

How much leaks out is not known. How much is safe to be exposed to is not known. What the effects of this are over time are not known.

"But how can you be sure there's no danger from radiation?"

A few things are known:

A. The farther you are from the video screen the less radiation you are exposed to. Radiation levels drop quickly with distance. A few inches from a video screen, a measurable amount of radiation is given off; several feet away, the amount is no longer measurable.

B. Color monitors give off more radiation — as much as five times more — than monochrome.

C. Radiation is not good for you.

I remember looking at a sign in front of a building on my first trip to Los Angeles in the early 1970s. It said,

"UCLA CENTER FOR UNCLEAR MEDICINE."

I thought, only in Southern California would a medical center admit that there were any areas of medicine that were unclear; and to put it on a sign, and to devote a whole center to it — well, I was impressed.

A friend had to point out to me that the sign read UCLA CENTER FOR NUCLEAR MEDICINE. Since that time, I have been unable to look at the word NUCLEAR without seeing the word UNCLEAR.

The reports that have surfaced over the past ten years have only made it more unclear. Atomic bombs, meltdowns, nuclear energy, annihilation — did this perplexing subject have to pop out of Pandora's Box *on television*, too? Do we have to face major moral, social, and medical issues every time we turn on the TV or switch on the computer? I mean, can't they leave us *SCTV* and Space Invaders? Is nothing sacred?

A polling of the scientific community only heightens the dilemma. Some say radiation from video screens causes cataracts, miscarriages, leukemia, and arthritis, especially in the fingers because, on computers without detachable keyboards, the fingers are closest to the video screen for the longest periods of time.

"But I can't see any radiation."

Other scientists say that the chance a radioactive electron has of passing through the glass of a video screen is about the chance you or I would have of driving through Nevada with four feet of beachballs on the ground and a gallon of gas in the car. (I did not make that up. A nuclear scientist made that up. A man with credentials.) They say that even the sun gives off radioactivity, and that there is as much danger being exposed to daylight as there is to video light.

The more intricate the arguments, the more persuasive each side became. The only advice I could offer concerned computer users: use a monochrome video screen, and put it as far away from you as possible. (Yet another argument for the detachable keyboard.)

But then I wondered: should I be giving this advice at all? Maybe there's no danger to begin with. What's the point in scaring people? *The China Syndrome* was bad enough. No point in starting *The Computa Syndrome*. I was in the midst of deepening confusion when, suddenly, a solution appeared.

The Langley-St. Clair Company began marketing lead-impregnated acrylic screens that fit over regular video screens and block, according to Langley-St.Clair, 100% of all x-rays and most ultraviolet radiation. The acrylic, it turns out, was originally designed for windows in nuclear power plants.

I ordered one. It arrived, a sturdy piece of plastic, about a quarter of an inch thick; transparent, with a slight tint. It attached easily to my video screen with velcro tape. I felt safe from radiation, like Lex Luthor felt safe from Superman when wearing his Kryptonite-impregnated leisure suit. It was the magic shield of Gardol from my youth.

The only problem is that the acrylic screen reflects light almost like a mirror. Who wants to trade safety for annoying glare? (It's trade-off time again.) The Langley-St. Clair people readily admit the problem and, by the time you read this, they should have it solved. They plan to cover their acrylic with the Polaroid anti-glare screen mentioned earlier in the chapter. The whole package should cost around $100. (If they don't have it, their regular screen is about $50 and Polaroid's is around $70.) Not a bad price for no glare, improved video screen contrast, and peace of mind.

Well, those are all the drawbacks I've discovered about personal computers, except for unknowledgeable salespeople, lack of product support, and manufacturers arrogance and incompetence. But I'll discuss those in the chapters ahead. Besides, I never let those things stop me from having something I want. If I did, I wouldn't have a telephone.

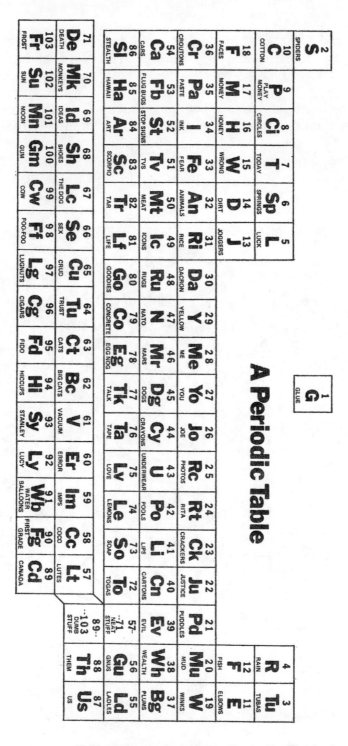

You can use T.K. Atherton's handy Periodic Table in selecting your personal computer.

Chapter Fourteen
Selecting a Personal Computer

Whenever I hear the words "selecting" or "choosing," I am reminded of a piece I read in *Daily Variety*. "Johnny Mathis 'coptered to his Irvine Meadows concert, but when the chopper refused to start-up after the show, Mathis chose to be driven home by car to L.A."

He *chose* to be driven home by car to L.A.? What, do you suppose, were his other choices? Riding a bicycle? Hitchhiking? Moving to Irvine Meadows?

If you are in the market for a personal computer and you only have $100 to spend, your choices are about as narrow as Mr. Mathis's. If you have $300-$400 to spend, your choices broaden. If you have several thousand to spend — or, rather, invest — the selection, and selecting, can be almost staggering.

My first piece of advice is, don't take it all that seriously. If you buy a personal computer now, and you like it, chances are* you'll be buying another one within the next few years. Most gourmet cooks are on their second or third Cuisinart. You may not like hearing this, just as car buyers in the early 1900s on the verge of buying their first car would not like to have been told that they would own ten or fifteen more cars during their lifetimes...but most of them did.

Still, you should choose your first personal computer carefully. Your first experiences with your first computer will invariably color your views of personal computers and computing for some time.

There are three factors to be considered when buying a personal computer:

1. What you want to use the computer for.
2. How quickly you want to do that on a computer.
3. Your budget.

Let's look at each of these points individually.

---

*One of my favorite songs, Johnny. Honest.

1. What you want to use the computer for. Although it's the program that determines what a personal computer does, certain personal computers run some programs better than others.

Personal computers fall roughly into two camps: those that process and display characters (letters and numbers) well, and those that process and display color graphics (spaceships and bar graphs) well. In general, the two are mutually exclusive.

One reason is the processor. Most processors in most personal computers are either designed — or at least utilized within the computer — to process either graphics or characters. This limitation is true of the current marketplace and will not be true a few years from now. The IBM Personal Computer, for example, is equally adept at handling either color graphics or characters.

Another reason is the limitation of the color video monitor. Color monitors, even the best, do not display letters and numbers as sharply as monochrome monitors do. This is likely to remain true for some time. Heaven knows millions of dollars have been spent on sharpening the image of color TV screens and no one — remembering the round, fuzzy pictures from the first color televisions — can deny that vast improvements have been made. It remains true, however, that even after these many millions invested and vast improvements made, the monochrome display is still sharper than the color.

Not that you can't process words and numbers on a color screen, or play graphic games on a monochrome screen — you can — but you will be happier, in the long run, processing characters on a personal computer designed for characters and processing graphics on a computer designed for graphics.

This division in personal computer design comes from the same two camps that nurture personal computers today: home and business.

The personal computer in the home is basically an entertainment device. Several personal computers can trace their ancestry back to the crude video games of the early 1970s. (Remember PONG?) They grew into computers aimed at the average American consumer, and this usually meant careful attention to color graphics. Even when characters were later added, the characters had to be in color. (Most people had just gotten color TV. *Nobody* wanted to go back to black & white.)

The personal computer in business is an ongoing miniaturization of the monoliths of the 1950s. It was a major breakthrough in business computers when a company no longer needed a climatically-controlled computer room. By the time a business computer was small enough to fit into an ordinary *closet*, well, that was something. To a business, the mere fact that data could be displayed on a *screen* — any screen — and not require a teletypewriter printout, was more than enough. Color? Who needs color? When the color green came to office video screens, that was plenty.

So the home/hobbyist computer continued to grow, and the mainframe/business computer continued to shrink, and today they're both getting close to the same size, and that size is recognizable as the personal computer.

It's an eventful time, rather like the driving of the golden spike that connected the railroads of the East and West. Like the Transcontinental Railroad, one group of computer manufacturers began (the home/hobbyist group) in the West and another group of computer manufacturers (the mainframe/business group) began in the East, and they're coming together in terms of size and philosophy somewhere out there in the Midwest, each hoping to capture the heartland of America.

There's no *reason* it started on both coasts and moved in. It could have, like broadcasting, started in the middle and moved out. (Network radio started in Chicago, and eventually moved to New York and L.A.) But moving in it is, and if you're going to be selecting a personal computer in the next, say, year — prior to the Japanese invasion (known affectionately among American computer manufacturers as "Pearl Harbor II") — it's good to keep these origins, and their differences, in mind.

So, if you want to use your personal computer to play graphic games, balance your checkbook in full color, and teach a young child the alphabet, you are in luck — there are several fine computers that do all of these well.

Or, if you want a computer for word processing, accounting, and displaying up-to-the-fifteen-minutes-ago stock market prices, you, too, are in luck — there are many fine computers that do these things as well.

If, however, you want to play full-color graphic games *and* process words, or do full-scale accounting *and* teach a young child the alphabet, you will have to select your computer more carefully and either (a) make compromises, or (b) spend more money.

2. How quickly do you want to do that on a computer? The world of personal computing is changing so rapidly that, every day you wait, the personal computer you eventually buy will do more and/or cost less.

This has always been true of technology. Light bulbs, when they were first introduced, cost a dollar. That was back in the days when people were making about ten cents an hour. Although light bulbs are a dollar again, people make more than ten cents an hour.

It's how badly you want the new technology, and how much it will do for you, that determines if you should buy now or save later.

In 1975, I bought one of the first video recorders offered for the home market, a Betamax. Each tape recorded for an hour. The timer turned the machine on and off, once, in any 24-hour period. It cost about $1,000.

In 1976, I bought a Betamax II. This recorded for two hours, allowing me to record entire movies while away from home. The timer, still, turned on and off once during any 24-hour cycle. It cost about $1,000.

In 1980, I bought a Betamax III. It recorded for up to five hours. I could set the timer to record four different programs on four different channels over a fourteen-day period. It had a remote control switch that allowed for fast forward (no more commercials), rewind (instant replays), slow motion, and freeze frame. It cost about $1,000.

Were I to buy a video player today, I could have all of the above features, plus eight hours of recording time, wireless remote control, and portability. What would it cost me? Oh, about $1,000.

And so it has been and will continue to be with personal computers. If someone were to ask me about my early purchase of a video recorder, "Don't you wish you would have waited?" I would reply with an unconditional "No." I feel I got a thousand dollars' worth of use out of the first Betamax, and certainly more than a thousand dollars' worth of use out of the second and, thus far, more than a thousand dollars' worth of use out of the third.

But that's me. I use it a lot and enjoy it a lot, and I do not feel that $3,000 for the past seven years' worth of use is unreasonable. I do not, however, feel that I need eight hours of recording, or wireless remote, or portability. Although I'd use them if I had them, they're not worth $1,000 to me. But they might be to someone else. I cannot, just because I happen to love and adore my personal computer, recommend that you run out and buy one. I use mine every day. You might not.

I gave my mother my first two Betamaxes and, in the past seven years, I doubt if she's used them twenty times. I gave her a phone answering machine. It seems to make a nice telephone stand, but it never gets turned on. If I were to give my mother a personal computer, it might be used as a nightlight, but that's about all. My mother has no real need for personal computers. Pizza, yes. Personal computers, no.

My brother, on the other hand is, like me, a writer. He spent three years writing stories on the computer at the newspaper where he worked. Now that he's moved to the Big Apple, he could use a computer to process his words with. (My mother and I bought him one for his birthday.)

If you have a need for a computer, but are waiting for prices to go down, buy the computer now. What you get from the computer as it fills your need will more than balance whatever saving you may gain by waiting. If you don't have a need for a computer, you can get it sooner or later, and it may not make much difference.

3. Your budget. Personal computers are available from $100 to $5,000. That's quite a range, and there are quite a range of features within that range. Which computer to get, or to get a computer at all, will depend on what you have to spend.

For example, a Timex/Sinclair, for $100, will attach to any TV and display words and symbols in black & white. You can, among other things, write and run BASIC programs on it. For $300 you can get a VIC-20, which has a color display, a much better keyboard, and far more adaptability. You get much more computer for $300 but, for many people interested in computing, $100 is already stretching it.

At $4,995, the Victor 9000 is a superb computer: two disk drives, monochrome video screen, detachable keyboard and yet, for $1,795, you can get a terrific computer, the KayPro II: two disk drives, monochrome video screen, and detachable keyboard. For a small business, the Victor 9000 is a bargain. For a struggling writer, the KayPro II is a blessing.

Personal computers, like cars, offer everything from transportation specials to limousines.

Before purchasing a personal computer, many people try to figure out which computer manufacturer will be in business five or ten years from now. These might be the same people who bought a DuMont television back in the early fifties.

I wouldn't spend a great deal of time wondering about that. Nobody knows. Here, for example, are some of the cars that were on the market in 1927: Ajax, Auburn, Buick, Cadillac, Chandler, Chevrolet, Chrysler, Cleveland, Dodge, Durant, Erskine, Essex, Flint, Ford, Gardner, Gray, Hudson, Hupmobile, Jewett, Jordan, La Salle, Locomobile Jr. 8, Maxwell, Moon, Nash, Oakland, Oldsmobile, Overland, Packard, Paige, Peerless, Pontiac, Reo, Rickenbacker, Star, Studebaker, Velie, Willys-Knight, and the ever-popular Whippet-Overland.

Do you think you could have selected one of the eight cars from this list that would still be manufactured 55 years later? And, if you could have, would it have made any difference?

The gold rush is on, and California is again its focal point; only this time it's not Sutter's Mill but Silicon Valley that draws the prospectors. "Computers or Bust!" More than one company has staked its corporate stick on some aspect or other of the microprocessing world. (If this book doesn't make it, *I'm* up a creek, and it's not Sutter's.)

There will be an alarming increase of computers and computer companies, followed by a leveling off, followed by a winnowing out. There will be bankruptcies, buy-outs, and mergers. (Shugart and Radio Shack forming Shugart Shack; Victor, RCA, and Vector forming RCA Victor-Vector; and maybe even Timex/IBM.)

You'll note in the above listing of automobiles the absence of Toyota, Datsun, and Honda. What about the "invasion" of the Japanese? Some people like to think, and voice their thoughts rather loudly, that American superiority in the field of computers is unsurpassable — even though more than half the printers sold in this country are made in Japan, as are a goodly percentage of the microprocessors, transistors, and other electronic innards of "American Made" personal computers.

Besides, The Big Three computermakers are acting more like The Big Three automakers every day.

Apple is using Ford's plan to advertise away all problems. The Apple II and Apple III are, dollar-for-dollar, not very good values. However, Apple's advertising campaign would have you believe you are paying a bit extra for *quality*. (Ford: "Quality is Job #1.") The fact is that, with the Apple II, you are paying for a computer design that is six years old — ancient by personal computer standards — and, of course, the ads necessary to keep it selling. Apple is planning, I hear, to introduce a new line of personal computers. They should have come out years ago.

Atari is like Chrysler. A good chunk of Chrysler's income comes from repackaging and marketing Japanese imports. A good chunk of Atari's income comes from repackaging and marketing one Japanese import in particular, Pac-Man.

Like General Motors, Radio Shack is the more conservative and financially secure of the three. On the whole, however, a Radio Shack computer is about as interesting as a Chevrolet. They both sell well, but so what? One day, right in the middle of *Good Morning America*, the consumers of this country will wake up and yawn, and that will be the end of GM and TRS.

Commodore has found a good thing in the VIC-20, and American Motors has found a good thing in the Renault, and they're both running with it. Beyond that, I don't know what either one of them is doing. I find their confusing array of cars and computers incomprehensible.

Maybe ironically, and maybe not, it's old Big Blue, ultra-conservative IBM — so slow to respond to a rapidly changing marketplace that they've been the butt of jokes around small computer circles for years — who seem to be offering the only real and dynamic challenge to foreign competition in the personal computer market.

They started from scratch, and using sound research and engineering principles, built a fine computer. They are marketing it in an aggressive yet intelligent way, with advertising that is attractive, informative, and understated.

I do not own stock in IBM; I do not even own an IBM. In fact, I sold my IBM (Selectric) to buy my personal computer. If you would have told me two years ago that I would be writing good things about IBM, I would have told you you were crazy. IBM has always represented to me the worst aspects of Big Business. Now I only have AT&T to dislike.

I have simply been watching, with a cool and dispassionate eye, the way IBM introduced and has supported their Personal Computer, and I am impressed. Unfortunately, we do not have an American auto company that parallels IBM.

So, don't pick a computer based upon how long you think the company might last. The list of computers changes monthly — certainly yearly — and ten years from now we will all laugh at the funny-sounding computer names, and the old timers among us will tell tales of how they once knew somebody who actually owned one.

And expect the Japanese to be here soon, in great numbers, offering the same quality at low prices that they have already brought to automobiles, electronics, cameras, and even steel.

Let's look at the basic component parts of the personal computer from a buyer's point of view.

Microprocessor

There are basically two types of microprocessors in personal computers today: **8-bit** and **16-bit**. Most personal computers are of the 8-bit variety, although an increasing number of 16-bit machines are being introduced.

Sixteen-bit microprocessors are more powerful than eight-bit, and more than just twice as powerful.

To illustrate, imagine a calculator that was capable of displaying eight columns of binary numbers. (See *Chapter Two*.) The value of the column at the far left would be 128. If, however, the calculator were extended to include 16 columns, the value of the far-left column would be 32,768. I don't know if there's a technical term that compares the relationship between the number 128 and 32,768. A non-technical term would be "significant."

Although this isn't exactly what goes on inside of a microprocessor, the example is given to illustrate that 16, in the world of computers, can be more powerful than "twice eight."

The use of 16-bit microprocessors is still in its infancy, and the potential they offer has yet to be tapped. Most software available for them is simply quickly re-written versions of 8-bit programs.

For the present, the major benefit of 16-bit computers is that the user-programmable memory can be increased. The maximum amount of user-programmable memory (RAM) an 8-bit machine can handle is 64K. For some programs, the ability to access 128K or 256K of memory is desirable, but unfortunately, not possible on an 8-bit machine. With a 16-bit machine, it is.

The fact that there is so little software available for 16-bit machines has prompted peripheral manufacturers to come out with plug-in cards that turn 16-bit machines back into 8-bit machines. This is rather like the phonographs back in the fifties that played both 78s and 33s.

For the present, an 8-bit personal computer is more than sufficient for almost all computing applications. In fact, many people buy 16-bit machines (the IBM Personal Computer and Victor 9000, for example) because they like the screen or the keyboard, not the microprocessor. Since the personal computing world is more comfortable with 8-bit computers, more than one person has told me of the IBM and Victor, "I wish this were an 8-bit machine."

For 8-bit machines used for the display and processing of words and numbers, the most popular microprocessor is the Z-80. The Z-80 allows the use of CP/M, the most popular operating system for non-game computers.

Operating Systems

While we're on the subject of CP/M, we might as well discuss operating systems. "Operating system" is a shortened version of **Disk Operating System**, also known as **DOS**.

A disk operating system simply tells the computer how to store information on the disk, and how to retrieve stored information from the disk. For the most part, the operating system is transparent to the user. The user is involved with running a specific program, and the computer runs the DOS to let it know how to interact with the disk drives.

If you take the computer-is-like-the-phonograph-and-the-program-is-like-the-record analogy from an earlier chapter, you can look at the operating system as the *kind* of record being played (78, 45, 33), and the specific program (word processing, accounting, spreadsheeting) as the *contents* of the record (Beethoven, Bowie, Draper).

It is only important to know about record formats when you buy a phonograph and when you buy recordings. To purchase a phonograph that only plays 78s might have been a good investment forty years ago, but it wouldn't make much sense today. Almost all records are either 33s or 45s, and you purchase a phonograph accordingly. When you're actually playing a song, it's impossible to tell if it's coming from a 45 or a 33.

The disk operating system on a computer is very much the same way. Once you are running a program, you would be hard-pressed to tell which operating system you were using.

However, the choice of operating system for personal computers is far more complicated than the choice of which phonograph to buy. In terms of operating systems for 8-bit machines, there's CP/M, and then there's everything else.

Apple has its own operating system. Radio Shack has its own operating system. Commodore has its own operating system. And so on. Selecting an operating system is not like choosing between 78s and 33s; it's like choosing between records, cassettes, 8-tracks, video disks, video tapes, microcassettes, and all the other possible methods of playing back recordings.

For some, the choice is made because of the programs available in a specific format. If you like the software offered for Apple, you must get the Apple operating system. The programs in TRSDOS (Tandy Radio Shack Disk Operating System) will not run on anything but a machine operating under TRSDOS.

For others, the choice will be based upon the machine. If you really *like* Commodore, then you use the Commodore operating system and choose your programs from the library of Commodore software.

For business, the choice is usually CP/M. A great many machines run CP/M, and the CP/M library is vast. CP/M, however, is not good at the graphic games many people want their personal computers to play. For most business applications, though, you'll find CP/M your best choice.

Then there are the 16-bit machines. There are only two major operating systems for 16-bit machines, IBMDOS and CP/M-86. CP/M-86 is the 16-bit version of CP/M. IBMDOS is IBM's disk operating system. Both are (of course) incompatible, so the race is on. IBM seems to be winning, simply because it's selling more 16-bit computers than anyone else, and every IBM comes with IBMDOS. (The Victor people are not taking sides: each Victor 9000 comes with both CP/M-86 *and* IBMDOS.)

It's an unfortunate situation. If you want the games of Atari and Apple, you'll have to buy an Atari *and* an Apple. It's rather like RCA selling records that will only play on RCA phonographs and Columbia is selling records that will only play on Columbia phonographs.

181

Disk Drives

Disks come in two sizes: 5¼-inch and 8-inch. (Although Sony is beginning to market a 3½-inch disk. Stay tuned. Film at eleven.)

5¼-inch drives are the most popular in the world of personal computing. They're more compact and easier to handle. A 5¼-inch disk can hold from 72K to 640K of information, depending on the computer. (K stands for kilobyte, or 1,024 characters. A double-spaced, typewritten page holds about 2K. To roughly figure disk capacity in pages, divide the number of K by two. 72K equals approximately 36 pages, 640K equals about 320 pages, and so on.)

The amount of disk capacity you'll need will depend upon the kind of programs you'll be running. Some programs, such as accounting, require large disk capacity, and may necessitate a hard disk. For most other business applications, 150K per drive should be considered a minimum.

The question then arises: Should I get one disk drive or two? For almost any business application, two is necessary. The need to make back-up copies of disks is crucial and, although copies of disks can be made on one-drive machines, it's much easier and faster with two drives.

For home use — storing BASIC programs and playing games — one drive of about 100K should suffice. Drives cost upwards of $300, and most homes could find better places to spend the cost of a second drive. One disk drive is recommended, however. Cassette tapes as a medium for storing computer information are slow, limited, and prone to error. Disks, by comparison, are fast, sure, and reliable.

Now, are you ready for some more confusion? Almost every manufacturer of personal computers has its own *format* for storing information on disks. This is not the same as the disk operating system, which tells the computer how to get at that information. The disk format is the way the information is stored physically on the disk by the disk drive. (I warned you it got more confusing.)

Returning to our phonograph analogy (talk about wearing out a record), let's say that the disk operating systems were 78s, 33s, and 45s. One record manufacturer may, for example, start the groove near the spindle, so that records play from the inside out. Another manufacturer may start the groove in the middle, play to the end, then pick up the arm, go to the beginning, and play to the middle.

And so it is with disk formats: everybody's got a different one. So, even if a program were written onto a disk using the CP/M disk operating system, it would probably not be compatible with any other computer, even if that computer were designed to run CP/M. A disk made in a NorthStar Advantage could not run on a TeleVideo 802 or a KayPro II or a Heath-89 — even though all four machines use 5¼-inch disks and can run CP/M.

Why this floppy disk Tower of Babel I will never know. There has been some talk about finding a standard for 5¼-inch disks, although it hasn't gotten very far. There is a standard for 8-inch disks, however — the IBM standard. (IBM invented floppy disks, but were, at the time, primarily interested in the 8-inch format. The 5¼-inch format fell into the hands of several microcomputer manufacturers simultaneously, and they each developed incompatible systems. Maybe it's all continuing today out of some sense of *tradition*.)

There are ways of transferring disks from one machine's format to another, providing that they are written in the same operating system. This can be done by some computer stores and costs about $20 per disk.

Keyboards

Membrane keyboards should be eliminated unless (a) money is tight or (b) you almost never plan to use the keyboard. On an Atari 400, for example, if you're using joysticks and playing games most of the time, you might never touch the keyboard except to answer the question, "Do you want to play again?" To push an occasional "Y" or "N" does not require an elaborate keyboard.

If, however, you want to do programming, typing, budgeting, or any other tasks requiring more than a flirting pass at the keyboard, avoid membrane keyboards.

When we examine keyboards that have movable keys, we find two different kinds: the cheaper-feeling keyboards

An Apple II keyboard

A TeleVideo 802 keyboard

and the more expensive-feeling keyboards. Cheaper keyboards feel, well, cheap. You get the sense that the keyboard design was not of primary concern to the designers of the computer, and it's clear that no one walked around saying, "Cost is no object!" when it came time to manufacture.

Other computer keyboards have a firm, solid feel to them. They were obviously designed for people who would spend a great deal of time working at a keyboard — writers, secretaries, accountants. You'll see what I mean when you compare the keyboards of, say, an Apple II with a KayPro II, or a Radio Shack III with a TeleVideo 802.

If you do little with your keyboard — use it to communicate with a data bank or record personal bank balances — the keyboard is not a major concern. If you plan to do some work at your keyboard — writing, accounting, even programming — select your keyboard as you would a spouse: you'll be spending a lot of intimate time together.

If you plan to do accounting on a personal computer, a numeric keypad is a must. This is a square of keys to the right of the regular keyboard that allows one to enter numbers quickly and easily.

For a variety of reasons given in the last chapter and the next chapter, a detachable keyboard is important if you plan to spend much time in front of your computer.

Video Display

Personal computers use two kinds of video display: **monitors** and **TV sets.**

Some computers use a device known as an RF generator to broadcast a signal to your TV. This little generator costs about $5. When you consider the millions spent on equipment by TV stations to get a sharp, clear picture into your home, you can imagine the quality of the picture produced for $5. It's OK, but not great.

Monitors, on the other hand, plug directly into the computer. They produce sharper images than do RF-generated TV pictures.

Be careful when you look at computers that use your TV set for the picture display. Often these computers are demonstrated using color monitors, not ordinary TV sets with RF generators. Many people have been disappointed by the images on their TV set once they got the computer home.

Another thing to be aware of is the penny-wise-pound-foolish possibility inherent in using your home TV. It seems logical to assume that, since one already has a TV, one might as well use it for a display. This is true — if you live alone.

What some people fail to consider, however, is that the TV cannot be used for anything else during Computer-time and, contrary to the Atari ads, the entire family will not want to gather around the TV *every night* and play video games. Occasionally, someone's going to want to watch *Happy Days*, and the battle for the control of the set is on.

The typically American four-TV-four-person household need not worry about this. They might, however, worry about the sharpness of the images, and that is another matter.

To play games, images do not have to be sharp. If a spaceship is a little fuzzy or the line of a maze is a little out of focus, people don't seem to notice. It's the action and the color and the movement one is concerned with.

When working with words and numbers, however, the fuzziness on the screen can be annoying.

One may wind up investing in that $300 monochrome or $850 color monitor after all — only to discover that the computer they bought so that they could save money by hooking it up to the TV doesn't produce the greatest letters and numbers anyway.

Some computers display only 40 characters across the screen. This is known as a **40-column screen**. Some produce 65 characters per line (a 65-column screen), while others produce 80 (an 80-column screen). Forty-column screens are OK for, say, reading classified ads on The Source or programming in BASIC, but for any serious letter-writing or accounting, 65 columns should be considered a minimum, and 80 columns are highly recommended.

Some computers, too, do not display uppercase and lowercase characters, just uppercase. Unless one were doing nothing but sending telegrams, any sort of writing on the computer would require both.

As touched on in the previous chapter, monochrome displays are sharper than color displays and are recommended for everything but color games and graphics. It is said that green phosphor is easier on the eyes than black & white.

In the next chapter we'll look at a few computers currently available; then, in *Chapter Sixteen*, we'll talk about making that great trek into the computer store and, finally, purchasing a personal computer.

As T.K. Atherton's drawing illustrates, a personal computer may or may not speed up scientific research/

Chapter Fifteen
A Name-Brand Buying Guide

This chapter is incomplete and obsolete. Even as I write, computers are being introduced and improvements being made on personal computers already on the market.

When all makes and models are accounted for, there are something like 200 personal computers on the market. This does not include software, printers, or other peripherals.

To spend just one day with each of these computers would take me the better part of a year, and to devote but one page to each of them would take the better part of this book.

I am reminded of a *Ripley's Believe It or Not* item from my childhood. It said that if the population of China were to line up and march four abreast past a point, the line would never end. Their rate of reproduction was faster than the number of people moving past the point. (I wondered, precocious youngster that I was, how they could reproduce that fast while standing in line.)

Reviewing computers, I fear, would have the same effect. By the time the 200 days were done, there would be another hundred computers to look at, and by the time I got through those, it would be time to start all over with revisions and improvements.

During all the days spent with these machines, of course, this book would not be in your hands. I postponed the publication of **The Word Processing Book** twelve times. Every week I heard about something new, and every week I thought, "I'd better investigate this — it's worth waiting a week if I can include it."

Three months later I had to draw the line: "What I know about word processing *today* will encompass the first edition of the book, and that's that."

And so it is with this book. What I know about personal computers right now is what will be in the book. I have more to learn than ever. Please do not consider me an expert. Think of me as, say, a friend of a friend, and hold my recommendations in that light.

Naturally, this information will change over time. You are welcome to write and ask for periodically issued Updates on personal computers. More about this at the end of the chapter.

Please don't let me, or anyone, select a computer for you. Personal computers are, above all, personal. What one person likes, another person dislikes; what one person finds annoying, another person might not notice. Like buying a car, you'll have to "test drive" a number of computers before you can comfortably decide, "Yes, this is the one for me."

At best, I will place before you a computer or two that you may not have considered before.

One final warning: these "reviews" are subjective and heavily biased. This chapter is nothing but my opinions and, just because they happen to be bound within the pages of a book, gives them no more credibility than any one else's.

An Introduction to the Symbols Used in This Chapter

The International Association of Computer Reviewers and Publishers of Books and Magazines and Other Materials About Both Computer Hardware and Software Being Manufactured All Over the World at Such a Rapid Rate (I.A.C.R.P.B.M.O.M.A.B.C.H.S.B.M.A.O.W.S.R.R.), in their eternal search for brevity, have created a set of Universal Symbols for Computer Reviewers and Publishers of Books and Magazines and Other Materials About Both Computer Hardware and Software Being Manufactured All Over the World at Such a Rapid Rate (U.S.C.R.P.B.M. O.M.A.B.C.H.S.B.M.A.O.W.S.R.R.).

Computers speak a universal language, and it is only fair that those who must write about computers should have a library of Universal Symbols at their disposal.

Peter A McWilliams
De Facto President

I.A.C.R.P.B.M.O.M.A.B.C.H.S.B.M.A.O.W.S.R.R.

Double-sided disk drive

 Computer will perform marriage ceremonies

 Computer plays synthesized dance music

 Suitable for a family

 Suitable for a rather strange family

 Suitable for a large family

 Suitable for a hungry family

Large file capacity

 Word processing capabilities

 Sold door to door by former encyclopedia salespersons

 Sophisticated

 Suitable for a couple

 Suitable for a rather strange couple

 Suitable for a couple who mess around

Suitable for a divorced couple

 Suitable for a male chauvinist

 Large memory

 Small memory

 Conforms to industry standards

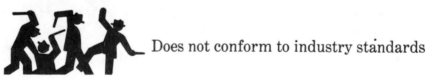 Does not conform to industry standards

Apple

Pair (Two disk drives)

 Palm (Made in California)

 Peanut (Word processing program approved by Jimmy Carter)

 Lemon

 Turkey

 Fishy

 Multiplies fast

Stinks

 May drive you to drink

 For the birds

 Portable

 Semi-portable

 Normal size video screen

 Small video screen

Large video screen

 Very large video screen

 Costs a lot of dough, boy

 If you need to ask, you can't afford it

 Build it yourself

 Not designed for human beings

 Electronic mail

Do whatever is necessary to get this computer

 Confusing

 Gives off a lot of heat

 Save your money

 Hot

 Not so hot

 Not hot at all

Video games available

 Realistic video games

 Trashy

 May put you to sleep

 May make you sick

 Has no idea what times the planes arrive

 Six out of seven people want this computer but can't afford it.

Timex/Sinclair

Clive Sinclair is one of those Britishers, like Freddie Laker, who wants to bring to the masses the playthings of the rich. For Freddie Laker it was transatlantic travel. For Clive Sinclair, it's personal computers.

For almost three years, Sinclair has been selling by mail a computer that was far less than anyone thought computers could possibly sell for. If it broke, you put it in an envelope, mailed it back, and they sent you a new one.

Timex, of course, is the company that, many years ago, decided watches should not be the exclusive domain of jewelers. They sold watches for far less that anyone thought possible. If it didn't work, you mailed it back and they sent you a new one.

Now they have joined forces, these two: the marketing might of Timex and the simple computer design of Sinclair — the Timex/Sinclair. They expect to sell millions of them. They probably will.

There are TV commercials planned. John Cameron Swayze is on a firing range. He straps a Timex/Sinclair to a target. The marksmen shoot, shattering the plastic case. A scientist in a white lab coat walks over to the

Timex/Sinclair and computes the value of pi to the 32nd decimal point. Swayze looks into the camera, holding up the battered remains of the Timex/Sinclair. "The Timex/Sinclair," he says. "Takes a shooting but keeps on computing."

Someone has called the Timex/Sinclair the world's first disposable computer. They may be right. I'm not sure how long anyone over the age of fifteen will use this computer before either (a) buying a better computer, or (b) giving up on personal computing altogether.

The computer has a smaller-than-full-size membrane keyboard. It plugs into any TV, although the display is limited to monochrome, even on a color set. The ability to do BASIC programming is built-in, as are 2K of RAM. Programs can be entered through the keyboard, or loaded through a standard cassette player (which you supply).

A printer ($100) saves what you've programmed, although the print-quality is, in a word, bad. An additional 16K of memory is $50. A modem, which allows one to contact The Source or CompuServe, is $100.

For a young person fascinated by programming (as opposed to the arcade games), this would be a frequently-used possession.

The VIC-20, at $300, features a full-sized keyboard, push-button (as opposed to membrane) keys, color display, arcade games, and much more. It's a better inexpensive computer, but for many, $300 may be too much.

I have mixed feelings about the Timex/Sinclair. On one hand, I'm glad that this much computing power is available for people — particularly young people — who can't afford more. On the other hand, I'm afraid that too many people will buy one, play with it for a week, and abandon the concept of personal computing altogether. These same people, had they invested in a better-quality machine, might have used computers daily.

As a way to contact The Source or CompuServe, it's quite inexpensive. However, if cost is a major consideration in computing, you might want to think twice about data banks. The minimum rate is around $5 per hour. (And that's after midnight. Most people, particularly young people, will want to use data banks during the evening hours, at almost $8 per hour.) Time flies on data banks and, like long distance phone calls to a lover, they can quickly add up. One could spend on data banks in a month the cost of a Timex/Sinclair with modem.

The programs offered for the Timex/Sinclair are varied and numerous, and likely to become more so. (For the most part, the programs come printed in a book. One copies the program into the machine and saves it on a cassette tape. When one wants to run that program again, he or she simply plays the tape. It's an awkward, but economical, procedure. Some people enjoy it.) There's even — Heaven help us — a word processing program.

The Timex/Sinclair will be well supported, simply because there will be so many of them around. It's fun. It's cheap. But comparing a Timex/Sinclair to some of the other more powerful personal computers is like comparing a Harley Davidson with a moped.

Main assembly room for Timex/Sinclairs

Apple, Atari, Radio Shack, and Commodore

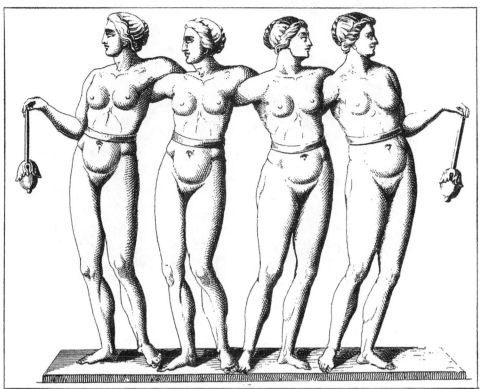

And a smooth-faced Atari executive, in charge of the Home Consumer Division, tears his gaze away from his in-office video screen and game master control to grin, "I play about 20 to 30 hours a day. If I had my druthers, I'd probably play all day long."—*San Francisco Examiner & Chronicle*.

The word Atari comes from the ancient Japanese game of GO. It's a board game, and when one player feels the surge of victory on his or her side, that player yells "ATARI!" The other player, struggling to avoid the "agony of defeat," might try any last minute maneuvers, but they usually fail. "ATARI!" is a cry of inevitable victory.

At the Atari Computer Company, each time favorable sales figures are released, all the employees go up on the rooftop and yell across the expanse of Silicon Valley, "ATARI!" At the other end of Silicon Valley, all the employ-

"Atari!"

ees of the Apple Computer Company respond by getting up on their roof and shouting, "SCREW YOU!" And the computer games continue.

I'm going to lump the four most popular computers together because I have basically the same thing to say about all four of them:

1. The computers are not so hot.
2. The support is terrific.

If you want to join a preformed, ongoing computer community, buy any of these machines. You'll find magazines, clubs, books, software, retail stores, and peripherals galore.

You may not wind up with the best computer, dollar-for-dollar, that you could have gotten, but you'll find a *family*. In some cases you'll find a cult, the members of which will be saying nasty things about me after reading this section.

I wish some great computers got the support that these machines have; or I wish these companies would come up with some great computers again.

I say "again" because, at one time, their computers were as good as any around, which is why they got so popular. Times have changed, and The Four Sisters have not changed with them.

The Apple II was introduced in 1977. That's not exactly what you would call "state-of-the-art," other than the art of preserving the past and selling it as the future.

The same is true of the personal computers marketed by the other three as well: What was a value in personal computers two or three or four years ago is ho-hum today.

And yet, it's because they've been around for several years, that there is so much support for them today. The more machines in the field, and the longer they're out there, the more programs and peripherals are offered — not only by the computer-maker, but by manufacturers of all kinds. Clubs form, magazines are published, books are written.

Like the chicken and the egg, the machines sell the software and the software sells the machines, and nobody is going to make obsolete the chicken that's been laying the golden eggs until the last moment.

And so, increasing amounts of money are spent on advertising, and a company leans a bit too heavily on its reputation.

For some, however, state-of-the-art technology is not as important as having someone to call when the program won't load — be it a friend who owns the same machine, or a fellow club member, or the salesperson who's been selling the same machine for so long that he or she knows it inside out.

For some, a monthly magazine (or two, or three) about nothing else but *their computer*, is more important than a sharper video display.

For some, a broad selection of programs more than makes up for a narrower selection of keys on the keyboard.

This selection of programs is especially important when it comes to full-color graphic games. These so-called

arcade games are available, for the most part, for the Atari and the Apple. Radio Shack with its Color Computer, and Commodore with its VIC-20, do have a selection of games — but if you want Pac-Man, it's Atari, and if you want Raster Blaster, well, you can run it on any computer you want, as long as it's an Apple.

(WARNING: Pac-Man on a coin-operated machine is not the same game as the home version of Pac-Man from Atari. Not only are the graphics sharper on the coin-operated version, but the game is more complex. Devoted video game players still play on coin-operated machines.)

I want you to be aware of the choice between support and state-of-the-art. There's only one computer company that seems to be building toward both, and that's IBM. (Discussed later in this chapter.) Unfortunately, IBM is on the expensive side, as home personal computers go.

If you choose one of The Big Four, you are choosing support. It's not a bad choice or a wrong choice. For many people entering the world of personal computers for the first time, it may be the best choice.

There is a great deal to learn when one gets his or her first computer. The more information available from a broad variety of sources, the easier learning that computer will be. That could be more important to you than 160 extra kilobytes of disk capacity for the same price, or a computer housing that isn't grey.

This is especially true if you live in a small town and your only contact with personal computers is a Radio Shack Computer Center, a computer store that only sells Apple and Commodore, and a department store that carries Atari.

Because there is so much written — books and books — about the computers made by The Four Sisters, I will not go into specific detail here. Each company has been promising, or let rumors circulate that it was promising, a new line of low-cost computers for the three years that I have been involved with computers. I hope these promises bear fruit in the near future. At that time I'll be happy to write a glowing review of a masterful computer at a low price with superb support.

Until that time, well, how about a few Apple jokes?

The Apple is highly recommended in some circles.

"Oh, I don't know. I was thinking more along the lines of an IBM . myself."

Of course, Apples are not for everyone.

"I will not buy an Apple, and get the hell out of here."

All right, I'll buy an Apple.

"Duh, an Apple, huh? Sounds good to me."

Many people are devoted to their Apples. Here a group of Apple owners worship the tree from which they believe the first Apple fell.

If you have the time, of course, you can grow your own Apple.

Or you can climb a tree, go out on a limb, and pick one.

"Can't we even bring the Apple?"

Franklin ACE 1000

If for some reason you feel you *must* buy an Apple II, you might want to investigate the Franklin ACE 1000. The basic ACE 1000 costs about the same as the basic Apple II, but includes a better keyboard (although, like the Apple, it is not detachable), a numeric keypad, and 64K of RAM. All of the plug-in cards, programs, and peripherals made for the Apple will work with the Franklin ACE.

The ACE is better suited to word processing than the Apple II (you can get almost every peripheral for the Apple but a new keyboard). The ACE, however, requires the plug-in card for 80-columns (like the Apple II, the standard is 40). The ACE requires a plug-in card for color.

The ACE is in fact so close to the Apple II that Apple is suing ACE. (Apple seems to be suing *everyone* these days. Why don't they come out with a line of great new computers and let everyone else imitate their dust? As it stands they're trying to get universal proprietary rights on 1977 technology. Why?)

For a better keyboard, and full Apple II compatibility, you might want to look at the Franklin ACE.

The Heath H-89

I put together my first Heathkit back in the summer of 1969. The United States had just placed a man on the moon, so I figured anything was possible. My knowledge of electronics was, as Bob Dylan might have said at that time, limited and underfed. I had changed a tube or two in an old television set and soldered a wire to a speaker once, but that was about it.

Heath, however, had a stereo receiver that had gotten top reviews in all the audio magazines. Heath promised easy, step by step, instruction. And the cost, in kit form, was far less than comparable receivers on the market. I accepted the challenge.

A week later, with no major traumatic incidents, the kit was assembled. I connected it carefully to my turntable and speakers, put on my favorite Doors album, and invited my roommates in for the grand unveiling.

The lights were lowered and the candles lit. I walked proudly over to my personally built Heath receiver, turned on the power, put the needle on the track, "This Is The End," adjusted the volume, and sat down.

No sound was coming from the speakers, but soon a stream of light blue smoke began coming from the Heathkit. My roommates, having no idea what I was up to, perhaps thought that I had spent a week building an electronic incense burner.

The tranquility of the blue smoke was replaced by yellow sparks and white smoke emanating from the rear of the cabinet. This was followed by a rather loud snap, and all the lights on my side of the apartment went out. Only the light of the flickering candles remained. All else was still.

We all sat in the darkness for a moment, not moving. The silence was broken by the voice of one of my roommates: "Far out, man," he said. Everyone filed out of my room, quite contented by the light show I had presented. I'm not sure they ever suspected that I had *planned* to play them some music.

The next day I drove to the Heath store in Detroit to discover the error of my kitbuilding ways. The technician took the receiver into his fold and returned to me a week later a perfectly functioning receiver.

I put together my second Heathkit last week. It was not a computer but, before reviewing the assembled Heath computer, I thought it only fair to spend a few hours building a present-day Heathkit. I'm glad I did.

I cannot tell you the solid thrill, the deep-felt sense of accomplishment I had from putting together that kit. It was a simple, "Two Evening" kit, and the satisfaction I found in putting the right resistor in the right hole and making a good solder connection surprised me. By the time the Two Evenings were up, six hours altogether, I had built my very own ultrasonic cleaner. It was mine. It was the focus of my care and attention for several hours, and I loved it.

Naturally, it didn't work. I say "naturally," not because notworkingness is the normal state of all newly-assembled Heathkits, but because, when an impatient writer goes messing around with capacitors and transistors and transducers, *naturally* he's going to screw something up. And I did. And the Heath people fixed it and returned to me a working ultrasonic cleaner that I built, but did not fix, myself.

I go on about kit-building because the fun of building a personal computer is one of the strongest things the Heath H-89 has to recommend it.

The H-89 is a fine computer; time-tested and reliable. The first H-89 was introduced in 1979. At that time it was a state-of-the-art personal computer, but in the past three years the competition has grown. The H-89 is comparable, and in most ways superior to, the Radio Shack TRS 80 Model III.

What the H-89 does offer that no other personal computer can is the satisfaction and pride that comes from having built it yourself.

The H-89 is a Z-80-based computer. In fact it has not one but *two* Z-80 microprocessors, one for the terminal and one for the computer itself. Since the terminal and computer do not share a microprocessor, in certain computing situations this could speed things up.

The screen display is a full 24 lines, with 80 characters per line. The keyboard has 80 keys, which includes a 12-key numeric pad. (Apple II has 48 keys and TRS III has 65.) The keyboard has a gritty smoothness to its operation; it feels as though it had been lubricated with graphite. The cursor keys are located on the numeric keypad above various numbers. This is unfortunate, because one must shift before each use of the cursor keys — an inconvenience. Discreet cursor keys would be an improvement. There are five programmable function keys. The keyboard is not detachable.

The H-89 comes with one disk drive built in. For programming, limited word processing, games, and electronic spreadsheeting, one disk drive is sufficient, although two would make copying disks much easier. For full-scale word processing, accounting, or other business related uses, two drives are a minimum. In terms of data storage, it is a quantum leap from cassette tape recorder to one disk drive; it is a similar leap from one disk drive to two.

The modest, built-in 100K of disk drive memory is expandable, in reasonable increments, to 11 megabytes.

Heath offers a full line of 5¼-inch, 8-inch, and hard disk external memory drives. Heath was among the first, in fact, to offer their users 640K of information on a single 5¼-inch floppy disk.

The H-89 has 48K of user-programmable memory (RAM), expandable to 64K, and there are three input/output ports. Very handy.

Heath is a hobbyist company, well established in the Do-It-Yourself tradition, and their catalog reflects this. To figure out the number of possible optional configurations of the H-89 would require, well, an H-89. If you want this, you must also order a that, and if you buy two thats, you get a special discount on one of these. However, if you buy one of these, you don't need the this, because this is included in these. And if you buy two of these, you can get one of them at half-price. All in all, if you can put together an H-89 system using the catalog, you should have no trouble putting together the H-89 itself.

In choosing software and peripherals, Heath chose wisely. The CP/M operating system allows the H-89 to run any of the thousands of programs currently available on CP/M. For word processing, they offer two of the best, WordStar and PeachText. In business software, the top of the line Peachtree programs. In dot matrix printers, again the best, the Epson MX-80. In letter quality printers, very near the best, Diablo. (Only the NEC Spinwriter could top it.)

Heath has their own operating system, word processing software, business programs, and dot matrix printers. They offer competing systems — on which they make less money — for one of three reasons: (1) They care about their customers and want them to have the best; (2) They know it's good business to treat customers well; (3) They know that if they don't sell the best, smart customers will buy it elsewhere. Romantic that I am, I like to think it's reason one.

A Heathkit Electronics Center is an interesting place. There you can learn the Ancient Arts of Ham radio, Morse code, and weather forecasting; or you can learn the more Modern Arts of direct-from-satellite television reception, solar hot water heating and, naturally, computing.

Heath sells all of these, plus high fidelity components, large-and small-screen TVs, metal detectors, log splitters, air cleaners, foreign language courses, auto accessories, radio-controlled model airplanes, electronic testing equipment, organs (of the instrumental variety), pinball machines, darkroom timers, telephone answering machines, electronic bathroom scales, burglar alarms, digital grandfather clocks, and more. With that many things to know a little about, don't be surprised if your local Heathkit Electronics Center salesperson does not know a lot about computers. And yet, beyond all odds, many of them do.

Unlike various other company-owned computer stores I've been to, the sales pressure at a Heathkit Center is low enough to be termed nonexistent. The salespeople are so laid back, in fact, that I've often thought the do-it-yourself quality of a Heathkit Center might extend to writing up your own order, ringing up your own sale, and making your own change.

Heath offers a full line of educational programs to supplement the computer. They have an extensive course that teaches the basics of microprocessors, microcomputers, and programming. It won the International Award from the Society of Technical Communicators, whoever they are. This course includes cassette tapes, a workbook, a flip chart of illustrations, and a kit for hands-on experimentation. On a less technical level, they have a course, with cassettes and workbook, that helps select the right computer for various business applications. They even have a course in Microsoft Basic (MBASIC) programming.

I found the BASIC programming course clear, concise, and informative; on a par with my ability to learn such things. To see how a younger, less experienced mind might take to all this, I loaned the H-89 and the course in BASIC to Rod, a 16-year old friend of mine, who had no previous knowledge of computers whatsoever. I called him a week later and asked him what he thought of the course. "It's pretty good if you're sort of stupid," he said.

He thought that the alternating male and female voices on the cassette tapes sounded like "...the recordings at the airport that tell you not to park in the red zone." He conceded, however, that learning how to program in BASIC had been worthwhile, but most of his time had been spent with Galactic Warriors. This is a version of Space Invaders, though more sophisticated, with seven levels of play. Try as I might, I could never get beyond Level Two. Rod was regularly playing at Level Five. After lamenting for a moment on what the younger generation was coming to, I thanked Rod for his feedback and hung up.

These courses, written for the mind of a 33-year old, but a bit sluggish for your average 16-year old, are available also for Pascal, COBOL, FORTRAN, and Assembly languages. These tutorials range in price from $49.95 to $149.95. For $39.95, they have a course in the Fundamentals of Personal Computing, which I promise to take before writing my next computer book.

―――――――

Heathkit is owned by Zenith, the company where "the quality goes in before the name goes on." The Zenith folks are the people who brought us the Space Phone, a device that allows you to answer your phone while watching television. The phone rings, you push a button, and the sound of the calling party comes from the speaker on your television set. It's such a modern marvel, I'm surprised that I bought a personal computer before purchasing my very own Space Phone.

Heath and Zenith work closely together in the area of computers. Zenith Data System products are sold through Heathkit Centers. The basic marketing philosophy seems to be: if it's assembled, it's from Zenith; if it's in a kit, it's from Heath.

The H-89 assembled, for example, is the Z-89, and the "Z," as I'm sure you can guess, does not stand for Zorro. The Z-89 retails for $2895, $1,000 more than the H-89.

If you want to learn about personal computing from the inside out, from microprocessor to programming, the H-89 is a good bet. If you want the pride and satisfaction of assembling your personal computer personally, the H-89 is for you.

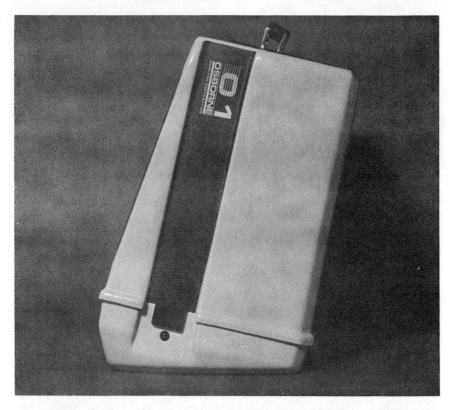

Folded, the Osborne 1 resembles a tipsy sewing machine

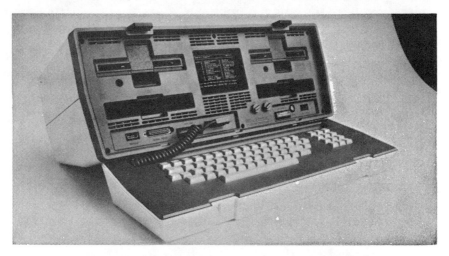

The new version of the Osborne 1, unfolded

The Osborne 1

I imagine that, several years from now, we will look back upon the Osborne 1 with the sense of fond amusement we currently reserve for, say, the first Ford, or the first $300 handheld calculators.

Folded, the Osborne 1 resembles a drunken portable sewing machine: the bottom of the carrying case is slanted and the unit, when standing on end, lists dramatically to one side. Unfolded, it looks like something out of Army Surplus. And the screen, the video screen, is *the smallest* thing you've seen coming out of an electronic box *that big* since the early 1940s.

However, its ugly duckling characteristics and other eccentricities notwithstanding, the Osborne 1 has a lot going for it. Z-80 Microprocessor, 64K user-programmable memory, and two 91K disk drives, all standard. Video screen, small as it may be, built in. Full-size, semi-detachable keyboard with cursor keys, alphanumeric keypad, and ten user-programmable function keys. RS232, IEEE-488, and modern Input/Output ports. Not only that, but the keyboard folds over the the screen and disk drives and the whole computer becomes portable. *And* you get software, software galore: CP/M, WordStar, MailMerge, SuperCalc, CBASIC, and MBASIC. All this, plus excellent documentation, for only $1,795.

I know. I shudder, too, before putting the word "only" in front of a figure like $1,795. It's a matter of value. If someone were to introduce a small car that was in almost every way comparable to a Honda Civic or a Toyota Tercel, but retail the car for $1,795, the word "only" might well apply. And that is very close to what the Osborne people are doing.

What does "Osborne" stand for? you might ask. IBM stands for International Business Machines, TRS stands for Tandy Radio Shack, an Apple is a fruit, but what's an Osborne? An Osborne is a real, living person named Adam Osborne. He is a computer writer turned computer book publisher turned computer manufacturer. He is not the father of Donny and Marie. He has the dubious distinction of being the first person to ever name a computer after himself. (With the Apple around, he didn't dare call it the ADAM.)

Mr. Osborne was known for an occasional enthusiastic attack on certain computers, and the entire computing industry at times, from his column, "The Fountainhead," in the magazine *Interface Age*. I'm sure that, more than once, an angry reader or manufacturer wrote and said "If you're so smart, why don't *you* try making a computer?" And that's just what he did.

His goal was to gather together the best of what already existed in microcomputing hardware and software and package these elements in a compact, low-cost, portable unit. Even his detractors would find it hard to deny that he has succeeded admirably.

The individual elements of the Osborne 1 were selected with business and professional people in mind. The Z-80 microprocessor, for example, is excellent for rapid manipulation of words and numbers, but poor in the sort of graphics display necessary for a good game of Space Invaders. 64K of RAM, and not one but two disk drives, was more than generous. The standard CP/M operating system allows the user to run literally thousands of pre-packaged programs.

In software, he continued his wise CP/M decision with WordStar and MailMerge, the most powerful word processing combination around. An electronic worksheet, SuperCalc, and not one but two forms of BASIC — MBASIC and CBASIC — round out an elaborate (and expensive: close to $1,500 retail) software package. From one point of view, you're paying only $295 for the computer. The areas in which Mr. Osborne (I guess I should refer to him as *Dr.* Osborne: he has a Ph.D. in Chemical Engineering) stayed within de facto industry standards and lowered the de facto industry standard price, his efforts did shine. However, when he wandered from the de facto straight and narrow, he did fall into the brambles.

Two examples come to mind. In duplicating the full computer keyboard he left out one very useful, and in some programs essential, key. This is the DELETE or RUBOUT key. Almost all business computer keyboards have this key. The Osborne does not. This is sorely missed if you've grown accustomed to using the DELETE key to remove the last letter (or word) typed while using WordStar, and some CP/M software uses the DELETE key to execute important functions of the program.

A far more dangerous straying from the path of de facto was the video screen. The standard video screen format for business applications is 24 lines, with 80 characters (columns) per line. Dr. O. got the 24 lines all right, but he missed the 80 columns by quite a margin. The screen of the Osborne 1 is just 52 characters long. A 52-character line is adequate, but marginally so.

There has been much talk in computerdom about the Munchkinesque screen built into each and every Osborne 1. Osborne claims it's a five-inch screen, but I've measured it every which way — vertically, horizontally, diagonally — and the maximum number of inches I have come up with is four-and-three-quarters. Now, we can't fault Adam for exaggerating a quarter of an inch. It seems to be a male prerogative.

It's easy to play Monday Morning Quarterback, and see how the O-1 might have been designed to hold a larger screen. First, the various input/output ports could have been placed in the rear of the machine, under a removable protective covering for travel. This would then get them out of the front panel, where they are mostly a nuisance. With a modem, a printer, an IEEE-488 peripheral, and the keyboard all attached to the computer with thick, flat cable, approaching the disk drives is almost as difficult as mating with a reluctant octopus. Further, putting most I/O ports on the rear of the machine would, once again, have been more in keeping with de facto standards.

Next, the disk drives could have been mounted horizontally and placed next to each other, leaving room for a seven- or eight-inch video monitor on one side. (This piece was written before seeing the KayPro II. As it turns out, by following the above suggestions, one would have room for *nine*-inch video screen. More about the KayPro II in the next review.)

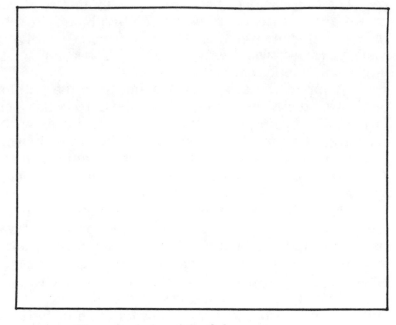

The actual size of the Osborne 1 screen

This sort of thing, of course, is easy to see when writing about other people's already-built computers, which may very well be what started Adam Osborne in the personal computer business. (Hummm. "The MCWILLIAMS 1." It has a certain ring to it, don't you think?)

Three other slight screen irritations:

1. When the disk drives stop or start, the screen image momentarily shrinks and flutters.

2. A piece of thin plastic covers the screen, to reduce glare, I must assume. This bit of plastic is very fragile and scratches easily.

3. The lines on the screen that I used went slightly uphill. This, combined with the fact that the computer, when shut and standing on end, lists to one side, gave me the sense that I might be computing in Pisa.

A 12-inch external video screen is available from Osborne for $250. This makes the type larger, but one is still locked into the 52-character line. "Soon," the Osbornes say, an adaptor will be available that will make the external monitor an 80-column screen, while maintaining the 52-character built-in format. This will be in the form of a circuit board, costing from $500 to $600. This same circuit board will, at no additional cost, turn both disk drives from single-density to double-density format. (The 91K is increased to 182K per drive.)

If you have a monitor, or want to use your television screen (or the television screen in any hotel room), an adapter is available from a company known as JMM Enterprises. JMM is a real person, too, James M. Morefield. He makes various "peripherals adapters" for the Osborne 1. One will turn the existing Osborne extension video jack into a standard video monitor jack. (Why Osborne didn't use a standard video monitor plug is beyond me.) This is known as a MONDAPT (Monitor Adaptor) and sells for $39.95. The MONDAPT II has an RF generator and allows any TV to become an Osborne 1 video screen. That one is $79.95. (The screen display of the last adaptor, I fear, is not very good.)

JMM also sells extension cables that make the keyboard truly detachable, in lengths from one to four feet ($29.95 to $49.95). The cable supplied with the Osborne is about a foot long, which is better than the keyboard being glued to the computer, as is the case with so many (too many) all-in-one computers, but is not quite long enough to comfortably sit on a lap. (A catalog of other JMM peripheral adaptors is available from JMM Enterprises, Box 238, Poway, California, 92604.)

My only concern about the disk drives is that the disks inside the drives get rather warm. This is because the Osborne 1 is cooled by convection and not by a fan. I can only surmise that disk life can be dramatically shortened being exposed to high heat for long periods of time.

In terms of noise, the lack of a fan is a real plus: when turned on and sitting alone, the computer is dead quiet. No hum of a motor or whir of a fan. It could sit on the edge of an executive's desk all day, silently.

The software has been nicely adapted to the Osborne. The cursor keys actually control cursor movement in WordStar. There is still more room for adaptation, however. The help data, the menu, and almost all information other than text (which can be set at a 50-character width to fit within the 52-character screen) spans a full 80-character screen. In other words, slightly less than half the information is off the screen at any one time.

There is a real advantage in buying an all-in-one, portable computer from a local dealer: if anything goes wrong, you can carry the unit in and say "Here, fix it." If various parts were purchased from various vendors, or if the whole thing was purchased from a vendor several thousand miles away, finding out what needs repairing, and then having it repaired, could be a nightmare.

The Osborne 1 had its share of technical difficulties at the start. These seem to be mostly corrected now. If you get an Osborne, it's a good idea to turn it on and leave it on for a week or two. This is known as "burning in." Most electronic parts that are going to fail will fail during this period of time. Without the burning in procedure, the parts will fail eventually, usually a week or two after the unit is out of warranty, or, in the case of a portable computer, somewhere in Kansas. The majority of the electronic parts that don't fail will last longer than you will.

A well-circulated ad for the Osborne 1 shows two men, one in a black suit carrying an ordinary attache case, one in a white suit carrying an Osborne 1. We are told that the man deprived of the Osborne 1 "doesn't stand a chance."

The dog-eat-dog undertone of this ad aside, there is an implication that the Osborne 1 will replace the attache case. For most businesspeople, it will not. Stacks of paper are still a necessary part of business, no matter how computerized one's company might be. To be more accurate, the man in the white suit would have the Osborne 1 in one hand (the stronger one) and an attache case in the other. If he used the Osborne away from available power sources, he would have a battery pack slung over his shoulder as well.

The word "portable" is a relative one. A 19-inch

television is referred to as portable, but only when compared to a 25-inch console. You wouldn't be expected to carry a dishwasher to a picnic just because someone deemed it "portable."

And so it is with the Osborne 1. When compared with every other full-scale computer on the market, it is portable. It is not, however, something you would want to carry with you from place to place with the same freedom you would an attache case.

According to the owner's manual, the Osborne 1 weighs 23.5 pounds. (The new case makes it one pound heavier.) Unless you're a cinder block salesman, it's doubtful that your attache case would ever grow to be quite that heavy. Although 23.5 pounds is not an impossible weight, you would need a computer quite a lot before you would add that much to your daily load.

It's also bulky. It's at least twice as thick as most attache cases. This means that it does not just hang from the arm as you walk, but must be held slightly away from the body or it bumps against the leg.

The Osborne people seem quite proud of the fact that the Osborne 1 will fit under an airline seat. I think that getting it *to* the airline seat will cause more trouble than fitting it *under* the seat. Considering the obligatory executive attache case, the Osborne 1 might well find itself traveling as checked baggage.

I would not, however, check the Osborne 1 as is. The plastic housing is simply not designed for the primate handling checked baggage receives. A well-padded electronics case, the kind made for cameras or video equipment, would protect the Osborne rather well, I think, and allow for curb-side check in and baggage area pick up. For less frequent trips, the original carton the Osborne comes packed in would work almost as well.

The portability of the Osborne is greatly enhanced by the fact that it works on both AC and DC power. This means that, with an adaptor, it can be plugged into a cigarette lighter and used in a car, or connected to its optional battery pack and used anywhere at all. (The battery pack will provide from one to two hours of power before recharging.)

Meanwhile, the Irish Republic is planning on placing Osbornes in the Irish school system. Just think: the next Wilde or Shaw or Brendan Behan might write his first bit of prose on an Osborne 1.

Osborne Issues Warning To Competitors: Expect Some 'Cherry Bombs' In The Way

SAN FRANCISCO — Adam Osborne, with typical self-assurance, celebrated the first anniversary of the introduction of his precedent-setting $1795 portable computer by issuing a warning to competitors who hope to share in his newly created market.

"I'm not foolish enough to think that we're going to own 100 percent of the market," Osborne said at the recent West Coast Computer Faire. "I welcome those who are in effect endorsing our concept, but business is business—they'll find I have a few cherry bombs in the way."

Osborne Computer Corp.'s press luncheon was ostensibly called to announce a double-density disk drive option and battery pack for the briefcase-sized system, but there was little focus on those features. With cameras from CBS-TV's "60 Minutes" capturing the news conference for posterity, the discussion centered more on the future than the present.

Commenting on his company's success, Osborne noted that imitation is the sincerest form of flattery. "We clearly expect a large number of competitors," he said.

"When you are involved in a systematic effort to eliminate the typewriter from the office, it's only natural."

Osborne said he could not be specific about plans for the immediate future, although he dropped plenty of hints. And foremost in his litany on the company's future was the gospel of standardization.

Osborne said that his company is developing a means to standardize disks, so that the Osborne I will be able to read disks written on other machines. "It's an idea whose time has come," he said, "even though others seem to be going in the opposite direction."

Osborne appeared to aim his comments at Apple Computer Inc., the company that still dominates the personal computer market. Osborne called Apple the "oddball of the industry," noting that the company will eventually have to change its strategy of independent software and hardware in order to succeed in the future.

After other officials wrestled with those questions for a while, Osborne broke the mounting tension with a response that affirmed his reputation as an industry gadfly:

"Assumption is the mother of all f---ups."

KayPro II

Move over Adam, Andy is here.

The Adam of my first sentence is, of course, Adam Osborne. The Andy of my first sentence is Andy Kay, a soft-spoken MIT graduate who, in 1952, manufactured the first digital voltmeter. Like Adam, Andy has invented a personal computer. Like Adam, Andy's personal computer is inexpensive and portable. Like Adam, Andy has named the computer after himself. Adam's computer is the Osborne 1. Andy's Computer is the KayPro II.

How do they compare? Put simply, as a personal computer, the KayPro II is superior to the Osborne 1 in every detail — yet it retails for the same $1,795. As David Letterman might say, "Unbelievable!"

The main disadvantage of the Osborne 1 is the screen size. The five-inch screen is so small that it permits only 52 characters per line.

The KayPro II comes with a built in nine-inch monitor. This may sound as though the KayPro II screen is almost twice as large as the Osborne 1. It's not. It is, in fact, due to some geometric law which I do not begin to comprehend, nearly *four times* larger than that of the Osborne 1.

That four-fold increase makes all the difference in the world. The KayPro II displays lines of characters that are large, sharp, clear, and 80 columns wide. (Both the Osborne 1 and the KayPro II display 24 lines.) The display on the KayPro II is, in fact, far more readable than an Osborne 1 with the $250 twelve-inch Osborne external monitor attached. The screen on the KayPro II is green phosphor, the built-in screen on the Osborne 1 is black & white.

While the characters on the screen of the KayPro II are sharper than the Osborne 1 — and easier to read than the display of the Apple II, Radio Shack III, Commodore VIC, or any Atari — the characters are still not as sharp and fully formed as, say, the TeleVideo 802 or the IBM Personal Computer.

The keyboard on the KayPro II is superb. Manufactured by Keytronics, it is the same keyboard used on far more expensive computers. It's rather like saying that Volkswagen will start putting Porsche engines in all VW's at no increase in price. The keyboard has a separate numeric keypad and separate cursor movement keys. (Even the IBM Personal Computer doesn't have those.)

The cursor keys of the KayPro II are individually programmable to meet the cursor movement demands of almost any program.

The KayPro II keyboard is detachable. It's connected to the main computer by standard telephone cord — the cord that goes between the handset and the phone. (The Osborne 1 requires the purchase of a special cable costing about $10 per foot.)

While the Osborne 1 has basically the same keyboard layout as the KayPro II, the feel of the KayPro II keyboard is firm and solid, while the feel of the Osborne 1 is, by comparison, springy and loose.

The KayPro II comes with two built-in 5¼-inch disk drives. Each drive holds 191K of information after formatting. This is more than twice as much as the Osborne 1's 92K per drive. Even after adding the $185 Osborne double-density option, The KayPro II holds more information per disk. (191K vs 182K.)

The central processing unit on the KayPro II is the ever-popular Z-80, and the user-programmable memory (RAM) is a full 64K.

Andy Kay's company, Non-Linear Systems, makes test equipment for engineers and the aerospace industry. They manufacture, for example, the world's smallest oscilloscope. Non-Linear Systems has packaged their personal computer with the ruggedness of a piece of electronic testing equipment.

The KayPro II has an all-metal case, faceplate, and keyboard base. (The keys coming out of the base are plastic.) If the KayPro II catches on, it could single handedly put the United States steel industry back on its feet. By comparison, the Osborne 1 is devoted to the continuing boom in the plastic and pressed fiberboard industries.

The new case for the Osborne 1 is a testament to the sleek lines of molded plastic. It is in neutral beige and has "OSBORNE" branded a quarter of an inch deep into the case. The KayPro II is in blue with "KayPro II" painted on the side. It has a fashionable Hi-Tech look. (KayPro 1, by the way, was a prototype unit and never marketed. In naming his computer KayPro II, do you suppose Andy is anticipating Adam's Osborne II by a few months?) If one *must* have plastic, the KayPro II offers an optional vinyl carrying case.

The new Osborne 1 is a pound heavier (aren't we all?), which brings it to about 24.5 pounds. The KayPro II weighs 26 pounds.

In working with the Osborne 1, I had a sense of flimsiness in construction. I felt I had to be very careful or something might break. The KayPro II gives the impression that it could take on Conan the Barbarian and rise victorious. It's built like a brick pagoda. Maybe it's the metal case (almost all other personal computers are plastic), maybe it's the no-nonsense design, maybe it's knowing that it's made by a company with thirty years' worth of experience in packaging delicate electronic instruments for portable use. Whatever it is, it's the only personal computer — at any price, portable or no — that I would describe as rugged. (The next closest would be the Horizon Advantage.) The KayPro II would be at home in Marlboro Country.

The input/output ports, as well as the on/off and reset switches, are cleverly located at the rear of the machine. (The Osborne has all but the on/off switch on the front plate, which is one reason why the video screen is limited to five inches.) The back of the KayPro II has a handle and becomes the top of the case for carrying. (The electrical cord wraps around four posts on the four corners of the back plate.)

The keyboard folds over the screen and disk drives and is held in place by two plastic (!?) latches. This forms the bottom of the closed unit.

The KayPro II comes with an RS232 modem port and a Centronics-type parallel interface. The printer default is the parallel port. A supplied program (CONFIG) will change the default port to the RS232 and switching pins 2 and 3 on the printer cable will permit the use of a serial printer.

The KayPro II is well-vented and designed so that no fan is needed. I left a KayPro II on 36 straight hours and the case didn't even get warm. The Osborne 1 gets warm. The Osborne 1 I was sent for evaluation got warm after only a few hours, and particularly warm (dare I say hot?) around the left disk drive.

The absence of a fan makes the KayPro II an ideal computer to use where absolute silence is required. The executive will find the combination of small size, large screen, and total silence an irresistible combination for a personal office computer. It will sit on the corner of a desk, silently, all day, taking up very little room. The writer who finds his or her concentration broken by the white noise of a fan will find the KayPro II a blessing.

Most Osborne 1 owners I've talked to think of their "Ozzies" as a respectable, inexpensive first computer that will serve them nicely until their ship comes in, or until full-size personal computer prices drop dramatically. Others think of the Osborne 1 as a reasonable portable computer, to be used "on the road" but not in the office or in the home. Most think of it as an acceptable second computer, or an inexpensive way station en route to a full-sized computer.

The KayPro II, on the other hand, is all the personal computer many people may ever need. The keyboard is good. The 9 inch-video screen, close up, is as comfortable to work with as most 12-inch monitors two or three feet away. The disk drive capacity is more than adequate. One may find themselves buying a KayPro II as an inexpensive, portable first computer — and never buy a second.

The KayPro II will not do graphics, in either monochrome or color, and it therefore will not play flashy computer games. It will not turn your house lights off at night or start your Mr. Coffee in the morning. Alas. It will, however, run any of the thousands of programs available in CP/M.

One of the drawbacks of the Osborne 1 is that, while it is a CP/M machine, the disk drives use   a format that is specific only to the Osborne 1, and not all software houses supply 5¼-inch disks in the "Osborne format." This means that one must buy the 8-inch format and have it transferred — at additional expense — or, in the case of some more complicated programs, do without.

Cleverly, the KayPro II people designed the disk drives to accept most CP/M programs available in the Xerox 820 5¼-inch single-density format. (The KayPro II and Xerox double-density formats are not compatible.) One buys the Xerox single-density 5¼-inch disk, copies it on the KayPro to another disk, and that's it. If the program needs to be installed, the KayPro II emulates the ADM3 terminal.

Using a supplied progam (TERM), the KayPro II becomes a dumb terminal that duplicates the operation of the ADM3. This allows the KayPro II to access larger computers or, with the addition of a modem, to tie into data bases such as The Source or Compuserve.

Adam Osborne began the Great Software Giveaway with the Osborne 1. With each Osborne 1 you get CP/M, WordStar, MailMerge, MBASIC, CBASIC, SuperCalc, and

A smart horse, answering the question: "What is the screen size of the KayPro II?"

a photograph of what Mount Rushmore might look like if Adam's head were carved into it.

Well, once again, KayPro II outdoes the Osborne 1. The software included with each KayPro II is the Perfect series of programs: Perfect Writer (word processing), Perfect Speller (spell checking), Perfect Calc (electronic spreadsheet), and Perfect Filer (a data organizer).

But that's not all. For the home they include three programs: Family Budget, Net Worth Statement, and Income Tax.

For a small business they include Income Statement, Cost of Goods, Expense Reports, Accounts Receivable, Accounts Payable, Invoice Entry, Cash Flow Assessment, and Payroll Analysis.

But wait! There's more! For the investor there are a series of programs to analyze stocks, real estate, professional fees, break even, and CHI-Squares. (Don't ask me what a CHI-Square is. All I know is that you can analyze one with a KayPro II.)

This is certainly the most impressive array of free-with-purchase software included with any machine at any price.

I asked Andy Kay the obvious question: Did he intentionally set out to knock the Osborne 1 off?

"No," he answered, "About two or three years ago I thought it would be good to have a portable computer for engineers. We've done a lot of work for the aerospace industry, and I thought a good, solid portable computer would go over well within the technical trade.

"About two months into the project someone came in with the announcement for the Osborne 1. We've followed the Osborne 1 closely, and decided that our computer had a broader audience than just engineers."

I asked him the other obvious question: Can you keep up with the demand?

Andy Kay thought for a moment. "We'll try hard."

"KayPro! Oh, I beg your pardon, Atari!"

Morrow Micro Decision

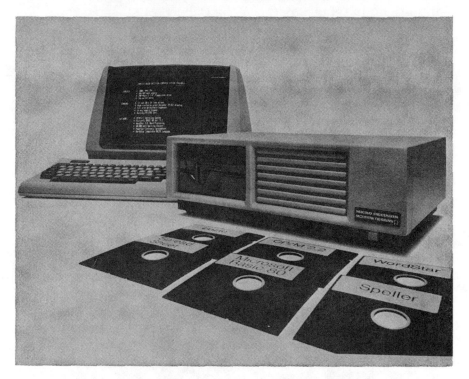

This is a fine computer and an excellent value.

The standard Morrow Micro Decision computer comes with one disk drive (186K formatted capacity); a 12-inch green phosphor screen (25 80-character lines); a Z80A processor; 64K of RAM; a detachable keyboard with a numeric keypad, separate cursor movement keys, and seven programmable function keys.

And that's not all: Morrow is a member-in-good-standing of the Great Software Giveaway Program. You get, free with purchase, CP/M, Pilot (a program that makes CP/M more friendly), WordStar, Microsoft BASIC (MBASIC), BaZic (for NorthStar compatibility), Correct-It (a spell-check program), and LogiCalc (an electronic spreadsheet).

All this for $1,790. One more 186K disk drive brings

the price to $2,140.

The screen display is sharp, clear, and legible. (On the prototype monitor I saw, the lines undulated ever so slightly. I'm hoping this will be corrected in production units.) The keyboard is solid, with a good feel. My only complaint, as a user, is the noise the disk drives make. Sometimes they sound like a subway braking, and at other times they sound like Darth Vadar breathing. I'm hoping that (A) the noises were only in the drives I listened to, or (B) not everyone is as delicate about the sound of disk drives as I am.

I first heard about the Morrow Micro Decision the way I hear about most things these days: a letter from a reader. This reader wrote:

"The company is MORROW DESIGNS out of San Leandro (California) and seems to be a well established producer of hard disks and S-100 type board components. DUN'S Directory tells me they have thirty-five employees and the listed officers are all named Morrow. I have traced their ads back to 1979."

I do believe I have the most wonderful readers in the world. I wrote back and told him he should consider working for *Sixty Minutes*.

I do not know how many employees Morrow has (I do know the boss is named Mr. Morrow), but I know they have a good reputation and have been around the computer world longer than I have. They are a solid company, and will no doubt stand behind their product.

However, it is a new computer, and the precautions that apply to any new computer do apply. As Fats Waller said more than once, "One never knows, do one?"

The Morrow Micro Decision is a great computer at a great price, and well worth your consideration.

Sanyo MBC 1000

The Sanyo is also a great computer at a great price. It is similar to the Morrow, except whereas Morrow gives extra software, Sanyo gives extra disk capacity. (186K per drive on the Morrow, 326K per drive on the Sanyo.)

The basic Sanyo includes one disk drive (326K); a 12-inch green phosphor screen (25 80-character lines); 64K of RAM; and a detachable keyboard with separate cursor movement keys, numeric keypad, and five function keys. Also included is CP/M and SBASICII.

The price is $1,795. An additional disk drive is $395. (The extra disk sits in its own cabinet off to one side.) This would bring the price of a two-drive system to $2,190.

The weak link of the Sanyo is the screen display. The characters are formed using only a 6x7 dot resolution, and the dots are therefore noticeable. The display, however, is far from intolerable, and better than, say, Apple II or Radio Shack III. (But not as good as Morrow.)

The Sanyo MBC 1000 is the least expensive, high disk capacity computer on the market.

The Otrona Attache

The Otrona Attache is everything the KayPro or the Osborne is, except better, smaller and, naturally, more expensive.

One gets two disk drives, each with 380K of memory; a 5-inch monitor that displays, sharply and clearly, 24 80-column lines; a green phosphor screen capable of graphics; and lots of software: CP/M, WordStar, Microsoft BASIC. All this in a package about half the size of the Osborne, and weighing only 18 pounds.

The cost? More than twice as much, $3,995. It is, however, the most portable personal computer today, and that degree of portability, plus its extra power, make it for some the perfect choice.

Escort

The Escort combines the portability of the Attache with the large (9-inch) screen size of the KayPro II. It does this by using the Sony 3½-inch MicroFloppy disk drives. These take up less room (and have less weight) than 5¼-inch drives. Two are built into the Escort (with a generous 322K per drive). The disk drives are quiet to the point of being silent.

The Escort costs the same as the Otrona, $3,995. That price includes CP/M, Spellbinder (word processing), Multiplan (electronic worksheet), and Microsoft BASIC.

The Teleram T-3000

The Teleram T-3000 (hereinafter referred to as the Teleram) is the most portable full-function computer available. It's perfect for people who travel a lot on planes or commuter trains. (I assume anyone who can afford that many plane tickets or a house in the country can afford a $2,995 computer.)

The Teleram weighs about nine pounds, has a full-function keyboard, and four eighty-character lines of display. The display is liquid crystal, like pocket calculators. While one would not want to write a magnum opus on a four line screen, it's surprisingly useable — far more so than the one-half line displays found in other portables.

The Teleram stores information on a bubble memory. Bubble memory is user-changeable, like RAM, but it keeps the information indefinitely, even when the power is turned off, like ROM. It's a great combination of the two, but, at the moment, fairly expensive. The $2,995 price includes 128K of bubble memory. An additional 128K is $600.

The batteries of the Teleram last about five hours before recharging. In the near future, an interface unit, disk drives, and a video monitor will be available. This would allow the Teleram to be used as a regular computer in the home or office, and a portable computer on the road.

243

Toshiba T100

The Toshiba personal computer includes a full-function keyboard, a monochrome (green) screen, Z80 processor, 64K of memory, two 280K 5¼-inch disk drives, and CP/M. All this for $2,480. Not bad.

The weak link in this system is the video display. Although an 8x8 dot-matrix character generation should be adequate, for some reason the letters look broken and spotty. This could just be the display of the unit I saw, or it might be inherent in the design. I would recommend comparing the video display quality with other comparably priced personal computers.

A positive aspect of the video display is that, with the simple addition of a color monitor, the T100 is capable of full-color graphic display.

Cromemco

The Cromemco offers a keyboard, monochrome (green) video screen, Z80 processor, 64K of memory, two 390K 5¼-inch disk drives, a "CP/M-compatible" operating system, a word processing program, a spreadsheet program, and a structured BASIC program. All this will cost you $2,380.

If you'd like to economize, you can leave off one of the disk drives, and the entire package would cost you only $1,785. A second disk drive can be added later for $595.

The keyboard, although detachable, is small and does not include a numeric keypad. The programs are Cromemco's Own. I have not had a chance to use them, so I cannot comment on them. Since they come free with a computer that is a a good buy even without software, if the software doesn't meet your needs, you can always buy a program that does.

Although this is a new computer, Cromemco has been making small computers for some time. Let's hope the bugs that so often plague new computers have been worked out in design and testing, and not in the marketplace.

This is a good, economical, and welcome addition to the world of personal computing.

The NorthStar Advantage

The NorthStar company began life, no kidding, as Kentucky Fried Computers. There was, back in 1976, a sense of whimsey in the world of personal computers. Today there's too much money involved for whimsey. When high finance comes in the door, whimsey goes out the window. (Or, as Groucho Marx put it, "When lust comes in the door, love goes innuendo.")

Soon Kentucky Fried Computers became NorthStar Computers, Inc.

The Advantage is ruggedly built.

I wouldn't hesitate putting this computer in front of someone who had learned how to type back in the days of upright manual typewriters, when to "bang out a story" was an accurate description.

What the Advantage gains in durability, however, it lacks in subtlety. I would not want to caress a poem out of the Advantage keyboard. Further, the Advantage keyboard is not detachable.

A non-detachable keyboard carries the idea of an all-in-one computer too far. Detachable keyboards have become the de facto standard for the latest generation of personal computers, and for good reason. Keyboards that are not welded to the video screen can be placed wherever the user prefers. The ability to move the keyboard wherever one wishes makes a personal computer more, well, personal.

A nondetachable keyboard is about as limiting as a car seat that cannot be adjusted. If you're an "average" driver you might never notice this inflexibility. If you're shorter or taller than the norm, you will find operating the machinery a study in discomfort.

There are 15 programmable function keys as part of its 87-key keyboard. Each function key has three levels of usage; hence, a total of 45 functions.

Businesspeople will be impressed with the Advantage graphics. Anyone who spends time creating pie charts and bar graphs — or wishes they had the time to create some pie charts and bar graphs — will find one program, Busigraph, worth the price of admission.

Having never worked with computer graphics before, I surprised myself by creating a pie chart within ten minutes and without reading a word of documentation. I spent the next several hours creating imaginary pie charts covering a broad range of subjects, some of which are not discussable in a book about computers.

Busigraph, a diagnostic system, and several graphics demonstration programs are included in the $3,595 price.

The graphics demonstration programs are enjoyable. One, called Kaleidoscope, creates random, never-ending patterns of light that range from striking to beautiful. It turns the computer into an art piece and a conversation piece all at the same time.

The screen display for graphics is a sharp 640 x 240 pixtels. (A pixtel is a little dot on the video screen from which graphic patterns are formed.) By way of comparison, the Apple III is 560 x 200 and the IBM Personal Computer is 640 x 200. The IBM and Apple III, however, are capable of full-color graphics, something the Advantage is not. The screen is green phosphorus. Pie charts, bar graphs, or any other graphics, can be printed using a dot matrix printer.

To write your own programs, or to run pre-written programs, requires the purchase of an operating system. The Advantage offers two: Graphics CP/M and Graphics BASIC/Graphics DOS. Each costs $149.

CP/M is, of course, the industry standard operating system for eight-bit personal computers. With CP/M you have access to a broad range of pre-written business programs. The NorthStar Graphics CP/M also allows you to program graphics, providing you know assembly language.

If you want to program graphics in BASIC, you'll need the Graphics BASIC/Graphics DOS software. This includes the standard NorthStar DOS and a form of NorthStar BASIC, GBASIC, that permits programming graphics. Anyone familiar with programming in BASIC should have no trouble adding the graphics commands to their programming arsenal.

When the video display is used to display letters and numbers, the Advantage is adequate but not superior. The character display is made up of a dot matrix pattern that is only 5 x 7. Compare this with the TeleVideo 802, which has a 14 x 10 character dot resolution. It's easy to see little dots making up the letters when looking at the Advantage screen. On the TeleVideo 802, the IBM, and the Victor 9000, one sees letters, not dots.

Two 5¼-inch disk drives are built in, each disk holding a generous 360K of formatted storage. NorthStar was among the first to use 5¼-inch floppy disks in computers, so one can count on their years of experience to produce a dependable, well-integrated drive system.

The Central Processing Unit is the time-tested, industry standard Z-80A, and an additional 8048 processor controls the keyboard and disks. The user-programmable memory is an ample 64K, with an additional 20K available for graphics display. The documentation is clear and complete.

Certainly anyone whose job involves making

numerous pie charts and bar graphs would clutch the Advantage to his or her bosom with enthusiasm bordering on passion.

In situations in which computers are used by a parade of uncaring and ungentle people, I would think the Advantage would last longer and perform better than any computer in its price range. This would make it an ideal computer for certain classrooms, businesses, and laboratories — the very market in which the NorthStar has proven so popular.

The Advantage is a well-constructed, full-featured computer with special appeal for educational and business applications. It is a worthy addition to the NorthStar tradition of fine computers.

NEC APC

NEC, the people who make the finest letter-quality printer around, make several small computers marketed by at least two different divisions. The one that seems to be getting the most attention is the APC, which stands for Advanced Personal Computer. As fond as I am of the NEC printers, I must admit I am not very fond of the APC.

The keyboard is solid, and the screen display is clear, but then so is the keyboard and screen display of computers costing half as much. The drives are 8-inch, and only 8-inch. They are also the noisiest drives I have heard on a small computer.

The processor is 16-bit. The software for the APC is limited, and there is no adapter card for running 8-bit software.

All this for $3,998. If it were $2,000 cheaper, it might be a breakthrough. As it is, it's not a great word processing value.

The strength of this machine seems to be when a color monitor is added. If sharp, full-color graphics are required by your business, you should certainly have a look at the APC. (And if you're someone who *must* do word processing in color, this would be a machine to investigate.) (The color monitor adds about $1,000 to the price.)

TeleVideo 802

The TeleVideo 802 is one of the best values in personal computing — and one of the best-kept secrets. The 802 is a great computer, loaded with features, with an excellent price, but has anyone ever *seen* one? Prior to this paragraph, did you know a computer named TeleVideo existed?

This name-brand recognition is important in the world of computers. People are running their businesses on Apple IIs or doing word processing on Ataris — Heaven help them — because, well, everyone's *heard* of Apple and Atari.

First-time computer buyers live in fear of a dialogue that goes something like this:

"I got a computer!"

"Great! What kind did you get? Apple? Atari? Radio Shack? IBM?"

"A TeleVideo."

"Say what?"

I don't know how a computer becomes a household word. However it happens, it has not yet happened to

TeleVideo.

The TeleVideo 802 is, however, a fine computer.

To build a personal computer, TeleVideo began with the best: their own 950 terminal. TeleVideo has been manufacturing high-quality, low-cost video terminals for years. The 950 is the top of a line of a dozen-or-so models. It has a detachable keyboard, 24 eighty-column lines, numeric keypad, 22 programmable function keys, etc., etc., etc.

Starting with an excellent keyboard and video screen, they added a Z-80A microprocessor, 64K of user-programmable memory, a CP/M operating system, and two 5¼-inch disk drives, each holding 340K of information. In every case, TeleVideo met or exceeded the de facto industry standard for personal computers.

The price of the TeleVideo 802 is $3,495.

If you want a computer for business or word processing — and you do not require graphics — the 802 is an excellent choice. It will run any program in the vast CP/M library. (The 802 is fully supported by Lifeboat, the largest distributor of CP/M software in the world.)

If, however, you require graphics for either work or play, you had better look elsewhere. The 802 will not, for example, play games of the flashy, full-color-with-sound-effects arcade variety. If you have Pac-Person fever, the TeleVideo 802 will not reduce it.

If you have a pile of correspondence to reduce with a word processing program or a pile of invoices to write with an accounting program or a pile of decisions to make with an electronic spreadsheet program, then the 802 will reduce, write, and make them — accurately and well.

Let's look at the individual components of the TeleVideo 802 and see why it's one of the best "serious" personal computers available today.

The keyboard of the 802 is excellent. It is, to begin with, detachable. A detachable keyboard allows you to place the keyboard and the video screen wherever you find each most comfortable. When the keyboard and video screen are welded together, a compromise on either screen placement or keyboard placement — or both — must take place.

The keyboard has a full "Selectric-style" placement of keys. The letters are large and clear. The feel of the keys is firm but friendly. (Don't ask me what friendly feels like. I read it in an ad somewhere and it seems to fit.) Everything on the keyboard is well-placed and convenient.

There is a numeric keypad — which is a must if the computer is to be used for accounting — and 22 user-programmable function keys.

The green phosphor video screen is sharp and clear. Each character is made up of dots in a 14 x 10 dot matrix pattern. This means that each individual character is formed on a grid of 140 dots, a number so generous that a friend described it as "overkill." The screen has 24 eighty-character lines, plus a 25th status line. TeleVideo's years of experience in terminal design and manufacture is evident in the screen and keyboard of the 802.

To the left of the screen are two disk drives. Each 5¼-inch disk holds 340K of information. (The ads claim 500K, but, once formatted, what one has is 340K. Formatted disk space is the only fair comparison.) The 802 is the second generation of TeleVideo computers. Fortunately, the bugs were worked out on the 801 series. The disk drives on the first 801s, for example, never turned off. They just kept turning and turning. In the 802 they rotate and stop, as needed.

The microprocessor is a Z-80A. What can one say about this popular, fast, and reliable 8-bit processor? Everyone from Apple to Xerox has used it, with satisfying results. No matter what direction personal computers might take, the Z-80A has a firm place in its history.

The 64K user-programmable memory is once again more than generous. It is the maximum available for 8-bit microprocessors. You will, therefore, never find a standard CP/M program that requires more.

The choice of CP/M as the disk operating system was a wise — and increasingly inevitable — one. There are more programs available for CP/M than for any other operating system. The CP/M disk, by the way, is included in the cost of the computer, not a $150-300 "option" required by so many — too many — computer manufacturers.

Maybe one reason why TeleVideo is not a household word is that the TeleVideo company has spent the past year courting the business user with their 806 and 816 computers. The 806 can support up to six terminals or work stations, while the 816 can support, yes, sixteen.

The 802 can stand alone as a computer, or it can be used as a work station for either the 806 or the 816. A business could begin with an 802 and later move up to an 806, using the 802 as a work station for the 806. This ability to expand should appeal to a growing business.

The least impressive aspect of the TeleVideo 802 is the documentation. It's poorly organized and not well written. It abounds with sentences like, "Each diskette has a magnetic coating on both sides, much like a phonograph record." How many phonograph records do you own with a "magnetic coating on both sides?"

The documentation is full of unintended humor. It makes for enjoyable light reading, providing you're not trying to figure out how to operate a computer from it. For example, on page 8 of the manual is a section entitled, *How to Unpack.* "...The documentation is enclosed in an envelope on top of the TS 802." In other words, one must read to page eight in the documentation in order to find out where to locate the documentation.

Another favorite sentence, "Excessive moisture or oil particles in the air will hinder the performance of the system." Oil particles in the air? The weather bureau gives relative humidity, but how does one go about finding out the relative concentration of oil particles? And what is an "excessive" oil particle?

All things considered, I'd rather have a great computer with poor documentation than great documentation with a poor computer.

And the TeleVideo is just that: a great computer. If word processing or running a business are your computer needs, you would do well to consider the 802.

Xerox 820-II

The Xerox 820-II is the revised version of the Xerox 820. It has a detachable keyboard with numeric keypad and separate cursor keys, black and white video display (24 80-character lines), 64K of RAM, and a Z80A processor. This basic unit costs $2,245.

Disk drives can them be added in 5¼-inch, 8-inch, and hard disk formats. Two 5¼-inch drives, with 360K of storage per drive, runs $1,450. CP/M is an additional $200.

This would put the price of a Xerox 820-II, configured like a TeleVideo 802, to $3,895.

Sales abound, however, in the Land of Xerox. Contact your local Xerox Store for the latest special.

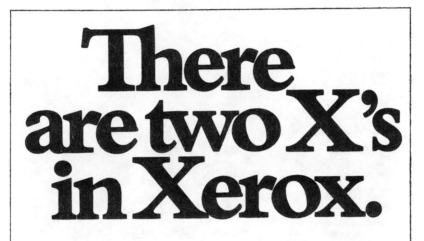

There are two X's in Xerox.

One on each end.

We're awfully tired of people spelling our name "Zerox" or "Zerocks."

It's "Xerox"—as in Xeres.

And, by the way, some of you insist upon calling photocopies made on Savin or 3m machines "Xerox" copies. Well, they're not!

Just cut it out. You think we want "Xerox" to become generic like "escalator"? So watch it. If we go under it's goodbye Masterpiece Theater and a whole lot of other good stuff on television.

The Eagle II

There is lots of good news and one piece of bad news about the Eagle II computer. First the good news:

It has a good keyboard, fine screen, Z80 processor, 64K of memory, two 360K 5¼-inch disk drives, and costs but $2,995. More good news: The $2,995 price also includes CP/M, CBASIC, UltraCalc spreadsheet, and the Spellbinder word processing program.

A good buy, that. A now for the bad news: It does not have a detachable keyboard. To quote Charlie Brown, "Arghhhh!"

The IBM Personal Computer

IBM has built, quite simply, a great personal computer.

Rather than patch together a small computer using a little from this IBM machine and a little from that IBM machine (which they easily could have done), IBM assembled a group of engineers, designers, programmers and, yes, a few personal computer lovers, sent them all to Boca Raton, Florida, of all places, and gave them a mission: Design and build the IBM Personal Computer.

They researched everything available in the field of small computers, investigated what was new, came up with a few things of their own, massaged the information together, made a few hard decisions, and created the IBM Personal Computer.

There was fear in the land of small computers that IBM would swallow up the personal computer market. Instead, it looks as though IBM has created a whole new industry. The industry is called, Supporting the IBM Personal Computer, Inc. Everyone's getting a franchise:

peripheral manufacturers, software vendors, mail-order houses, retailers — it's The IBM Personal Computer Bandwagon, and everybody's welcome to climb on board.

IBM is being unusually cooperative with people who want to make things that go in, on, or attach to the IBM. Prior to this, the firm corporate policy was: If it isn't made by IBM, it shouldn't be used on an IBM. Now IBM is releasing construction plans and detailed schematics of the Personal Computer, and offering help in every way possible.

They're even, wonder of wonders, marketing other company's products under the IBM name. The IBM printer is a Japanese-made Epson MX-80 with an IBM nameplate added. This is as radical as Steinway putting its name on Japanese-made pianos. At IBM it was unheard of — until now.

The Personal Computer is changing a lot of things at IBM, just as the IBM is changing a lot of things in personal computers. Prior to the introduction of the Personal Computer, IBM and personal computer owners had, at best, an antagonistic relationship.

Small computer owners thought that IBM was charging too much for their computers — they were marketing a desktop computer for $15,000, a machine that didn't do much more than $6,000 small computers at the time. IBM thought that the small computer people were inexperienced meddlers who, if they weren't careful, would give computing a bad name. Brickbats were thrown from camp to camp for years.

But, in the year-or-so since IBM introduced its Personal Computer, the wounds have begun to heal. Hardcore Apple users are considering, or actually buying, IBMs. Radio Shackers are turning over their precious, vintage TRS-80 Model I's to needy relatives and going IBM. And, even those who hang onto their home-built computers, are beginning to think that IBM's not so bad after all.

The Personal Computer is available in component parts. One can, for example, just buy the basic computer, plug it into a TV, and store BASIC programs on a cassette. Most people, though, who decide to Go IBM, go all the way: Monochrome screen, dual disk drives (340K per drive), 64K of memory, and detachable keyboard. This will set you back something in the area of $4,000.

The monochrome screen display on the IBM is excellent. Sharp, rock-steady, and nice to look at. It's green phosphor, with 24 80-column lines.

A color monitor can be added for high-quality full-color graphics. The arcade games are not yet available for the IBM in any great quantity, but they're coming, they're coming.

The keyboard is unique. Some people love it and some people hate it. This is because the IBM keyboard was designed with what is known as "audio tactile feedback." This means that when you push down a button on the keyboard, you *hear* and *feel* a click. This is not the same as the electronic beep or boop one finds as an option on some computers. This click is built into the keys. There's no way to switch it off or to get rid of it.

The idea is to give the typist both the sound and the feel of a key being struck. As I say, some people love it and some people can't stand it. Most people don't notice. Since the people who dislike it dislike it rather strongly, maybe IBM should offer a version "B" of their keyboard with no feedback whatsoever.

Another strange element of the keyboard is the placement of the SHIFT key. For years, small computer manufacturers who wanted to point with pride at the quality of their keyboards, referred to them as "Selectric-style." This meant that the keyboard had all the keys placed in the same positions as the IBM Selectric.

When the IBM designers made their computer keyboard, for reasons known only to the Creator and the creators, they did not follow the Selectric format. The SHIFT key on the left-hand side of the keyboard is traditionally the width of two keys and located directly next to the "Z" key. On the IBM Personal Computer keyboard, the SHIFT key is the width of one key, and *not* located next to the "Z" key. Further, the RETURN key is not as large as the RETURN key on a Selectric.

That the creators of the Selectric standard did not

follow that standard is something of a scandal in the land of small computers. (Listen, the computer industry's young. We don't have many scandals. Yet.)

Also, the keyboard does not have separate cursor movement keys. The cursor movement keys are located on the numeric keypad. One can use either the cursor keys *or* the numeric keys, but not both. This would pose more of a problem to electronic spreadsheeters, say, than word processors.

But, somebody's already introduced a keyboard that attaches to the IBM and corrects all these, uh, eccentricities. That's the nice thing about the IBM: It's likely to be the most supported personal computer in history. It almost already is.

Like the Apple II, anything you want to do on a personal computer, you'll no doubt find a peripheral or program that will let you do it. The Apple II, though, does it on the level of a high-school student. The IBM does it for adults.

IBM is a 16-bit machine. (See Chapter Fourteen.) This means that the software offered for it is not as broad as for, say, a CP/M-based machine. There is a solution, and a rather good one.

There is a card that plugs into the IBM called the Baby Blue. (IBM is known in computer circles, affectionately these days, as Big Blue.) This card adds 64K of memory to the machine (which, alone, would cost $540), a Z-80 microprocessor, and CP/M. It costs $600. This means that the thousands of programs written for 8-bit CP/M can run on the IBM, as well as the new 16-bit software being written especially for the IBM.

An example of software written especially with the IBM in mind is EasyWriter II, which turns the IBM into the closest thing I've seen to a dedicated word processor, at a fraction of the price. Other software manufacturers will be turning out software that makes use of the unique and powerful features built into the IBM.

The IBM's features have just begun to be tapped. It is a personal computer that will be around for a long time.

DEC Rainbow 100

In 1960, Digital Equipment Corporation (DEC) set the computing world on its ear by introducing a small computer at an outrageously low cost. Computing power had come within the reach of thousands more. The cost? A mere $120,000.

Today Digital is about to do it again, with a line of small computers that will put computing within the reach of thousands — perhaps millions — more.

These four machines are the Rainbow 100 (also known as the PC100), the DECmate II (also known as the PC200), the Professional 325 (PC325), and the Professional 350 (PC350).

The one I find most exciting is the Rainbow.

The Rainbow comes with a black & white screen that displays 24 lines of either 80 or 132 characters. (The screen switches easily between the two.) The keyboard is detachable and excellent. It ties with the TeleVideo keyboard as my favorite. (The *my* in "my favorite" is very important — you certainly might prefer others.) The keyboard is detachable. It has a numeric keypad (with add, subtract, multiply, and divide symbols), separate cursor movement keys, and more special function keys than one is ever likely to need (there are 36 extra keys on the keyboard).

The shift key, like on the IBM, is not directly next to the "Z." It is, however, larger than any other keys around it, and adjusting to the new placement is not a major hardship.

The disk drives are double disk drives, each holding two 5¼-inch disks. Each disk holds 400K of information, for a total of 800K.

The Rainbow is an 8 *and* a 16-bit machine. It will run either CP/M or CP/M-86 software. For $250 more you can run programs in the MS-DOS (IBM-DOS) format. 64K of RAM is standard. It is expandable to 256K

The cost is $3,495. Quite a value.

The word processing program chosen by Digital for the Rainbow is Select. I guess we can allow them one mistake. Actually, Select is a good choice for executives who type two letters per week, and maybe that's who they thought would be buying the Rainbow. I am also told the Select offered for the Rainbow is "enhanced." Well, for $595, the enhanced Select would have to be awfully enhanced. In the mean time, it's good to know that almost any word processing program will run, and run well, on the Rainbow.

A plug-in card permits high resolution graphics, and the addition of a color monitor with the card permits graphics in full color.

Digital gives away, for free, a book on personal computing (an embarrassment to those of us who *sell* books at $9.95 per. How would Digital like it if I started giving away *computers* for free?) The book is nonetheless recommended reading for anyone considering a computer — Digital or any other.

On the cover is a photo taken from high above an executive-engineer type, a keyboard sort-of on his lap. The man is looking directly at the photographer with a what-the-hell-are-you-doing-up-there? look on his face. Inside the book, for those concerned about Digital's solvency, is a photo of a building — only slightly smaller than the Great Wall of China — labeled "Digital Equipment Corporation, Parker Street facility."

You can write to them at Parker Street and request your copy. (*Digital Equipment Corporation, Media Response Manager, 129 Parker Street, Maynard, Massachusetts, 01754*) Ask for the book "Guide to Personal Computing."

DECmate II

The DECmate II is very much like the Rainbow, except that the processor is the Digital 6120, which is designed to run Digital's existing word processing program. It is (get this) a *twelve*-bit processor (just when I was getting used to eight and sixteen). But don't worry: for $495 you can have a CP/M auxiliary processor installed and run 8-bit CP/M programs just like everybody else. The CP/M plug-in card also adds an additional 64K of RAM.

The DECmate II, with the word processing software, is $3,745. This would give you a superior stand-alone word processor, for a fraction of the traditional Wang-Lanier-IBM Displaywriter (etc.) stand-alone price.

This is a top-of-the line word processing program, tailor-made for an excellent machine. It directly rivals the $8,000 to $15,000 stand alone word processors sold by The Other Guys. (Only a few months ago it *was* one of the $8,000 to $15,000 stand alone word processors!) It should certainly be considered if you're planning to spend more than $4,000 on your word processing computer.

The Victor 9000

The Victor 9000 is a superb computer. It's the-state-of-the-art for non-game playing computers.

The screen display is the best I've seen on a computer. Like the IBM, the characters on the Victor are made up of serifs — thicks and thins in the design of each letter. It looks more like printing than a computer display. Like the IBM, it has a green-phosphor, slow-phosphor screen that's sharp and rock-steady. The screen tilts up-and-down and left-and-right for maximum operator comfort.

The keyboard "solves" all the problems found on the IBM keyboard: The SHIFT key is large and located next to the "Z" key, the return key is massive; the cursor-movement keys are separate from the numeric keypad. Also, the keyboard is silent in operation. This will be good news or bad news, depending on your feeling about the IBM "audio tactile feedback." The keyboard is, of course, detachable.

The disk drives are 5¼-inch and hold a massive 640K each. (Expandable to 1,200K each.) 128K of user-programmable memory is standard. The price is $4,995.

The Victor, like the IBM, has a 16-bit processor. Like IBM, the Victor has a plug-in card that increases the memory by 64K, adds a Z-80 microprocessor, and allows the computer to run CP/M. The Victor card is known as the Victor-80 Card. It sells for $600.

While the Victor 9000 does excellent monochrome graphics, it will not do color graphics. It is also not likely to get the support that the IBM will be (and is) getting from the manufacturers of peripherals and software.

This means that, over time, the IBM will be able to do more than the Victor 9000. The things the IBM will do, however, may be of no concern to, say, a business.

For a business, the Victor 9000 is one of the best designed, beautifully packaged personal — sorry, desktop — computers available today.

The Victor 9000 is from the Victor Adding Machine Company, not the Victor Talking Machine Company.

Mother Earth News *is marketing a personal computer in the shape of a tree. Here a young couple use a light pen to check the price of soybeans on the organic commodities market.*

Updates

The information in this chapter is up-to-date (or as up-to-date as I can make it) through May 1, 1983. If you're planning to buy a personal computer some time after May 1, 1983, you are welcome to write and ask for whatever further comments I may have.

Please do not expect the Update to be a comprehensive listing of all personal computers that have come out from this time to that. It won't be. It will simply be a listing of computers and peripherals that I have been able to investigate in some way or another. It's just a letter from a friend of a friend.

This Update is free, although if you want to send a dollar or two to pay for printing costs, that would be appreciated.

Please include a **double-stamped self-addressed envelope** and ask for "Personal Computer Book Update #2." If you don't ask for "Personal Computer Book Update #2," it gets confusing. There are Updates for **The Word Processing Book**, and there may be Updates for other books. Also, there will be more Updates than just #2, so asking for #2 lets us know which one to send.

Update #1 has been incorporated into the buying guide of this edition, so there's no need to ask for that one.

You are welcome to write with specific questions, but I am very bad at writing back. I will, however, answer the questions of general interest in Updates, and incorporate them in future editions of this books.

Your comments are most welcome. They all will be read but, again, I cannot promise an answer.

If you'd like The Personal Computer Book Update #2, please send your double-stamped self-addressed envelope to:

Peter A McWilliams
Box 6969B
Los Angeles, California
90069

Thank you.

Chapter Sixteen

Purchasing a Personal Computer

Purchasing a personal computer will, for most people, require visiting a new kind of retail outlet: The computer store. Seven years ago there were no computer stores. Today, they're everywhere.

Please keep in mind that personal computing is in its pioneer days. You'll get along a lot better at computer stores if you treat them like trading posts on the frontier rather than as modern and sophisticated retail outlets.

When spending several thousand dollars on a consumer item, it is reasonable to expect some expert guidance, some personalized attention, and, yes, even a bit of pampering. At a computer store, feel lucky if they open on time.

A couple of years ago, there were only a few computer stores, owned and operated by knowledgeable, well-intended computer addicts who knew how to build, fix, operate, and program any computer in the store. There was only one problem with these people: they could not speak English. They had spent so long in the land of RAM that they were unable to describe life in anything but bytes.

All prospective computer buyer had to do was take a Berlitz crash course in Conversational Computerese and he or she was set. Once you learned how to communicate with the people in the computer store, in their language, you could find out anything you wanted to know.

Then the gold rush came. Someone took a look at the sales curve of personal computers and decided there was gold in them there hills. A great many someones did. Personal computers became the domain of entrepreneurs and investment bankers and venture capitalists and Wall Street. These people were in it for the buck, not for the love of computing.

And so the marketing was turned over to the advertising agencies, store designs to architectural firms, and sales to professional salespeople. These people knew how to speak English, but they didn't know beans about computers. Selling was selling, or so the theory goes, and if these people were good at selling widgets, they'd be good at selling computers.

Selling is a skill, just as knowing how to operate a computer is a skill, and I'm afraid there are precious few people in the world of computer retailing who know both. Computer merchandising is growing at such a rapid rate that if a person *did* know both, he or she would wind up as sales manager of the company within six months, *you'll* never see him or her on the sales floor again.

The fact that you will get neither stellar service nor sage advice from computer stores is nobody's fault, really. It would be nice to blame it on corporate greed or laziness or some recognizable evil, but I can't seem to find one.

The computer salespeople I have met are well-meaning and willing to help, they just don't have enough information *to* help.

Look at what they're up against:

1. Computers are changing all the time. If a store sells two or three different kinds of computers, one must know what's currently available, what's planned for in the near future, what peripherals are available, how each of these works, and what they do.

2. Further, one must know what the competition is doing, planning, marketing, and so on. A customer may come in and say, "I saw an ad for The Super Computer in *Time*. Why is your machine better?" A good salesperson should have a good answer.

3. Software is a jungle unto itself. Imagine being asked to know, in even a cursory way, something about every program in a given computer store, much less on the market.

Someone shopping for games might ask, "Do you have the game that's like *Dungeons and Dragons*, except that it has the Red Baron in cell number seven and the green tiger? I played it at a friend's house last week."

Someone shopping for word processing might say, "I need to do script formats, indexing, and footnoting, but proportional spacing is not necessary."

An accountant might ask, "Will this process receivables on a year-to-date or periodic basis?"

And so it would go for every software category. Computer people are not the only ones who have jargon.

4. It would help if the salesperson were a master of psychology. (Ph.D., with a minimum of three years' clinical experience, well-grounded in crisis intervention.) People have the strangest reactions when confronted with a world as unusual and different as computers. For some, the defenses rise to battlestation proportions. Others become so defenseless that they believe anything. Terror, disorientation, hostility. Sometimes it's hard to tell the difference between the waiting room at an out-patient clinic and a computer store.

5. Most people come to computer stores looking not for computers but *solutions*. This and this and this is wrong with my business, my children, and my life. Which machine will fix it, how will it fix it, and what will it cost? For a computer salesperson, the wisdom of Solomon seems to be another prerequisite.

6. Computers appeal to a broad spectrum of people, from pre-pubescents to post-doctoral candidates. A salesperson must be able to discuss programming with ten-year olds and video games with Nobel Laureates. If you're opening a computer store, you might check on the availability of Henry Kissinger.

7. After people spend $5,000 (or $2,000 or $3,000) on something, they expect *service*. "I didn't spend $5,000 on a machine to have it..." People can be awfully demanding.

People write me about **The Word Processing Book** *outraged* that I did not include a review of this-or-that computer, insisting that I write them back at once with my comments. My comments (although I've never dared write them) are that, if they demand that much from an $8.95 book, they'll never get $2,000 worth of satisfaction from a computer, so they might as well give up.

Naturally, the person who must carry the brunt of whatever dissatisfaction the customer might have is the salesperson. He or she must be, in other words, an expert troubleshooter, a crackerjack repair person, and a diplomat extraordinaire.

8. A salesperson also has to deal with the demands of his or her boss and the many manufacturers of software and hardware sold in the store. This takes the patience of Job and the integrity of Serpico.

One could begin to construct a picture, then, of the ideal computer salesperson. If you were to find such a person, you could easily get him or her elected President — or Pope. It is doubtful that, unless you came upon a Saint slumming it for a lifetime or two, this person would be selling computers.

The problem is that it's all so intricate and all so new, and it's getting more intricate and newer everyday. I don't know anyone who has successfully kept up with it all. I certainly don't pretend that I have. People pick an area and specialize: hardware, languages, games. I'm rather fond of word processing myself. You may have to talk to a lot of people in order to capture the gestalt of the whole thing.

There are ways of getting the most out of what computer stores have to offer. Here are some that I have found useful:

1. Make an appointment. Call the store and ask to speak to the expert in the field you are most interested in: accounting, games, word processing, electronic spreadsheeting. All you have to say is, "Which one of your salespeople knows the most about accounting?" When you reach this person, introduce yourself, and make an appointment.

Make it a specific appointment. They may try to get off the hook with, "I'm here every day from nine to five. Drop by anytime." Counter with, "Fine, how about Tuesday at three?" Call in the morning to confirm (i.e., remind them).

With an appointment, you are more likely to speak with the person who knows the most about the subject you are interested in, and you are more likely to get some specialized attention. Not much, but some.

2. Do not be intimidated by jargon. Salespeople who use excessive jargon are either from the Old School of computer selling and know everything about computers and nothing about communication, or they they are from the New School and know very little about computers but are trying to conceal that fact. When in doubt about what a word or phrase means, ask. Asking may not do you any good, but don't be afraid to give it a try.

3. Get some "hands-on" experience. Don't spend a lot of time discussing the philosophy of computing and looking at full-color brochures — sit down at a computer and *play* with the thing. There's plenty of time to talk while you're pushing buttons and watching the results of that button-pushing.

See if you can spend some time alone with the computer. This usually isn't too hard to arrange. When you have enough information to attempt a solo flight, all you have to say is, "Why don't you take care of some of your other customers and come back to me later?" There are almost always other customers to be taken care of.

4. Ask a friend who knows something about computers to come along. He or she will be able to tell you (later) whether the salesperson was giving you solid information or solid, uh, disinformation. They will also be able to, once the salesperson has gone, show you some great things about the computer. (Although don't expect your friend, who runs Program A on Computer B, to know very much about running Program C on Computer B.)

5. Use the computer for what you'll be using the computer for. If you're going to use it for creative writing, write something creative. If you're going to use it for correspondence, write letters. If you'll be doing accounting, do some accounting. If you're going to use your computer as an electronic spreadsheet, bring along some numbers and project some costs. If you're going to play games, play some games.

Different computers are good at different things. One that plays games well may be awful at business, and vice versa. (See Chapter Fourteen.)

"What do you mean overdressed? We're going to look at IBMs, aren't we?"

When you're done looking at your desired application, ask the salesperson to show you what else the machine can do.

6. Be on the lookout for good salespeople as well as good computers. If, while in the store, you observe a salesperson who really knows what he or she is doing, and it is clear that "your" salesperson does not, it is time for diplomacy, tact, and trickery. (Going from one salesperson to another is like changing dates after you're at the ball.) First, create some emergency that needs taking care of and leave. (You have to buy your seeds for National Potato Week or something.) The longer you stay in the store, the more the not-so-hot salesperson will feel you "belong" to him or her.

Exit soon, but first find out (a) the lunch hour and (b) the day of the week your original salesperson has off. (Make it sound as though you will rearrange your schedule so as not to miss him or her.) Return to the store next at (a) that hour, or (b) that day. The better salesperson should be on duty, and you now have a new salesperson.

7. Make notes. Write down model numbers, prices, salesperson's names, everything. After leaving the store, debrief yourself and note the pros and the cons of the machines and programs you've just evaluated. The things that are clear in your mind upon leaving a store will be hopelessly muddled a few weeks and a dozen computer stores later. Ask, too, for any printed literature the store can part with.

8. Trust your intuition. It's important that you feel good about the computer you purchase. Include your emotional reactions in your notes and in your decision. Just as cars are more than how many MPG they get, computers are more than how much RAM they have.

9. What happens if it breaks? Be sure to investigate what you'll have to do if the computer does not compute either in or out of warranty. Can you bring it back to the store or will you have to pack it up and ship it to California? How much time will repairs take? Are loaners available for free or at a reasonable cost? Will the store put all its promises in writing? Think about the unthinkable before you buy.

Although personal computers have proven quite reliable, I don't think we'll be seeing many ads like this in computer magazines.

"Now, over here is where we keep the printers."

10. Take your time. Don't try to look at everything in a week. You might experience a Personal Systems Overload. Take it easy. If you must travel to The Big City to do your investigations, it's better to plan several shorter trips rather than one long one. Gather all the information you can, let it digest, and make your decision from a relaxed state of mind.

11. Enjoy yourself. Keep in mind that it's hard to lose. All personal computers have *something* worthwhile to recommend them. To paraphrase Father Flanagan, there are no bad computers. You might not buy the best computer that fills your every need for the best price, but such is life. Whatever you do buy will serve you faithfully, teach you several magnitudes more about computers and computing than you know now, and assure that your next computer purchase will be an almost perfect one. Knowing there's no way to lose, enjoy playing one of the most intricate and challenging computer games around: buying a computer.

In getting the best price on your personal computer, it pays to shop the back pages of the various computer magazines (*BYTE* in particular). There you will find mail-order companies that sell computers at rather remarkable discounts. Some computers will be there, and some computers will not. Different computer companies have different policies, and although "fair trading" (i.e., price fixing) was ruled illegal some years ago, some companies control their dealers such that you can be sure you will never find one of their products sold for less than full retail price.

If the computer store in your area offers absolutely nothing in the way of knowledge and support, or if you live a goodly distance from even the closest computer outlet, you might consider buying a computer by mail. Most mail-order computer companies have good reputations, but the unspoken agreement is, "We'll sell you a computer cheap, but you're on your own after the sale." That means that fixing the computer is between you and the manufacturer (most are good at mail-in warranty repairs), and that learning the computer is between you and the Almighty.

*"Don't be afraid. There's nothing
in a computer store to harm you."*

If the computer store in your neighborhood seems to know what they're doing, can communicate that with a fair degree of intelligibility, and seems to be able to offer you after-the-sale support (a repair department, software, peripherals, maybe even classes), then buy from them.

You may or may not be able to get a lower price from the local computer store by showing them the ads in the magazines. They may give you a special "systems price," or throw in some software, or offer to come over to your house and set it up. Most stores, if they are interested in your business, will make some concession somewhere.

Don't expect them, however, to "meet or beat" the price in the mail order ad. The unspoken agreement between you and a walk-in computer store is that they will be there to serve you after the sale. This costs something, quite a lot actually and, like a club, you pay your dues when you join.

You might, too, consider hiring your salesperson, or someone you met in your quest for RAM, as a consultant. This is especially true in a business environment. Offer them $25 per hour — or more — to review your computer purchase just before making it, set the computer up, test it out, make sure everything is working, teach you (and your staff) how to run different programs, and be on hand to answer any questions as they arise (and believe me, they will arise).

If your consultant works, say, ten hours at this task, he or she might prove to have been the most valuable $250 peripheral you could possibly have purchased.

This brings us to an end which is, really, just the beginning. (Be careful. I tend to wax poetic and sentimental at goodbyes.)

It's been my pleasure escorting you through a small portion of this maze known as personal computing. I hope I have been of some help.

If you would like an update on personal computers, please write. The details are at the end of the last chapter.

Happy computing!

Appendix A

**An Illustrated Guide to
Selecting and Purchasing
a Personal Computer**

*More and more people are discovering the joys of personal com-
puting every day.*

Those who have not taken ample time in selecting their computer have had reason to regret it.

Get the advice of those who have trod the path of computer ownership.

Be sure to read good books on the subject.

Weigh the advantages and disadvantages of each computer system carefully.

Don't overtax your system by getting one too small to meet your needs.

Be sure to read good books on the subject.

Investigate the reputation of the store from which you plan to purchase your computer.

People who sell computers on street corners and back alleys are seldom reputable.

Find out if the purchase price of your computer includes delivery and set-up.

Be sure to read good books on the subject.

And even if you haven't read any good book on the subject, be sure to ask the advice of someone who has.

Be open to good advice from any source.

Even with expert guidance, it's easy to get in over your head.

After visiting a number of computer stores, you might want to go through the collected business cards and see which salesperson you liked best.

If you play your cards right, you'll wind up with a computer you can be proud of.

If you write anything from
a letter a day to a book a month,
reading this could change your life.

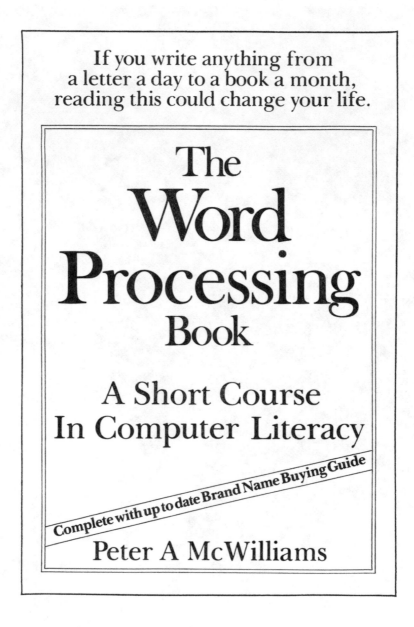

The
Word
Processing
Book

A Short Course
In Computer Literacy

Complete with up to date Brand Name Buying Guide

Peter A McWilliams

The companion volume to **The Personal Computer Book** is **The Word Processing Book**. If you are a writer, secretary, student, professional, or poet,   **The Word Processing Book** is recommended reading.

The Word Processing Book includes a name-brand buying guide of word processing programs, printers, peripherals, and personal computers, all from the word processing perspective.

The Word Processing Book is available (hopefully) wherever you purchased your copy of **The Personal Computer Book**, or you can order it by mail.

To order by mail, please send $9.95, plus $1.00 for postage and handling, to:

Ballantine Books
c/o Random House Mail Service
400 Hahn Road
Westminister, Maryland
21157

Or you can order by phone, toll free, and charge the cost of the book (plus shipping) to your Visa, MasterCard, or American Express.

800-638-6460
(In Maryland, please call 800-492-0782)

Please give them the ISBN Number of **The Word Processing Book** (345 31105-1) and the expiration date of your credit card. (If you would like to order additional copies of **The Personal Computer Book**, the ISBN Number is 345 31106-X.)

Please include sales tax where applicable and allow 3 to 4 weeks for delivery.

Thank you.

Addresses

Here, in no particular order, are the addresses of the manufacturers mentioned in this book.

Apple Computer
10260 Bandley Drive
Cupertino, California
95014
(408) 996-1010

Otrona Corporation
(Makers of the Attache Computer)
4755 Walnut Street
Boulder, Colorado 80301
(303) 444-8100

TeleVideo
1170 Morse Avenue
Sunnyville, California
94086

Smith-Corona
65 Locust Avenue
New Canaan, Connecticut
06840
(203) 972-1471

Radio Shack
Fort Worth, Texas
76102

Personal Computing
(Magazine)
4 Disk Drive (cute, huh?)
Box 1408
Riverton, New Jersey
08077

Creative Computing
(Magazine)
Box 789-M
Morristown, New Jersey
07960

IBM
Information Systems Division
Entry Systems Business
(I have no idea what the
last six words mean)
P.O. Box 1328
Boca Ratan, Florida
33432

WordPlay
Document Processing Center
(They rent word processors
   by the hour)
9037 Melrose
Los Angeles, California
90069
(213) 859-1221

Osborne Computer Corporation
26500 Corporate Avenue
Hayward, California
94545
(415) 887-8080

Epson America, Inc.
(Epson dot matrix printer)
3415 Kashiwa Street
Torrance, California
90505
(213) 539-9140

Sony Corporation
(Typecorder)
Office Products Division
9 West 57th Street
New York, New York
10019

Heathkit Electronics Corporation
(Heath H-89)
P.O. Box 167
St. Joseph, Michigan
49805

Zenith Data Systems
(Zenith Z-89—-assembled
version of Heath H-89)
1000 Milwaukee Avenue
Glenview, Illinois
60025

Xerox Corporation
Stamford, Conn.
06904
(203) 329-8700

Atari, Inc.
1265 Borregas Avenue
Sunnyvale, California
94086
(408) 745-2213

Interface Age
(Magazine)
P.O. Box 1234
Cerritos, California
90701

Non-Linear Systems
(KayPro II)
533 Stevens Avenue
Solana Beach, California
92075
(714) 755-1134

DynaType
(Computerized typesetting from
word processors through modems)
740 E. Wilson Avenue
Glendale, California
91206
213-243-1114

BookMasters
(Book printers)
830 Claremont Avenue
Ashland, Ohio
44805
(800) 537-6727

Xedex Corporation
(Makers of Baby Blue for IBM)
1345 Avenue of the Americas
New York, New York
10105

WP News
(A word processing newsletter)
1765 North Highland #306
Hollywood, California
90028

Commodore Computer Systems
681 Moore Road
King of Prussia, Pennsylvania
19406

North Star Computers, Inc.
14440 Catalina Street
San Leandro, California
94577
(415) 357-8500

Oasis Systems
(The WORD and The WORD Plus)
2765 Reynard Way
San Diego, California
92103
(714) 291-9489

Lifeboat Associates
(Software distributor)
1651 Third Avenue
New York, New York
10028

Ring King Visibles, Inc.
(Makers of disk storage files)
215 West Second Street
Muscatine, Iowa
52761
(800) 553-9647

MicroPro International
(WordStar and other software)
1229 Fourth Street
San Rafael, California
94901
(415) 457-8990

Peachtree Software
(PeachText and other software)
3 Corporate Square
Suite 700
Atlanta, Georgia
30329
(404) 325-8533

JMM Enterprises
(They sell adapters
  for the Osborne)
P.O. Box 238
Poway, California
92064
(714) 748-8329

Novation
(Makers of the D-Cat modem)
18664 Oxnard Street
Tarzana, California
91356
(800) 423-5410
(In California: 213-996-5060)

Discount Software
(Software at Discounts)
6520 Selma Avenue
Suite 309
Los Angeles, California
90028
(213) 837-5141

Dover Publications
(Publishers of the
Dover Archive Series)
180 Varick Street
New York, New York
10014

Select Information Systems
(Makers of Select and an
interactive tutorial on
how to use CP/M.)
919 Sir Francis Drake Boulevard
Kentfield, California
94904
(415) 459-4003

Langley-St. Clair
(they make the radiation filter
and market slow phospher video
screens)
132 West 24th Street
New York, New York
10011
(212) 989-6876

NEC Information Systems, Inc.
(Spinwriter letter quality printer)
5 Militia Drive
Lexington, Massachusetts
02173
(617) 862-3120

Muse Software
(Word processing for Apples)
330 North Charles Street
Baltimore, Maryland
21201

Small Systems Engineering
(makers of plug-in card for
Victor 9000)
1056 Elwell Court
Palo Alto, California
94303
(415) 964-8201

FYI, Inc.
(makers of SuperFile)
P.O. Box 10998
Austin, Texas
78766
(512) 346-0133

Lexisoft, Inc.
(Spellbinder word processing
program.)
Box 267
Davis, California
95616

Aspen Software
(Grammatik)
Box 339
Tijeras, New Mexico
87059
(505) 281-1634

Information Unlimited Software
EasyWriter II
281 Arlington Avenue
Berkeley, California
94707

Popular Computing
(Magazine)
P.O. Box 307
Martinsville, New Jersey
08836

BYTE
(Magazine)
P.O. Box 590
Martinsville, New Jersey
08836

The Source
1616 Anderson Road
McLean, Virginia
22102

Dow Jones Information Service
Box 300
Princeton, N.J.
08540

CompuServe
Tandy Corporation
Fort Worth, Texas
76102

Franklin Computer
(Makers of ACE 1000)
7030 Colonial Highway
Pennsauken, New Jersey
08109
609-488-1700

Morrow Designs
(Morrow Micro Decision)
600 McCormick Street
San Leandro, California
94577
415-430-1970

Bytewriter
125 Northview Road
Ithaca, New York
14850
607-272-1132

Dynax
(Distributor of
Brother printers)
333 South Hope Street
Suite 2800
Los Angeles, California
90071

Daisywriter
3540 Wilshire Blvd.
Los Angeles, California
90010
213-386-3111

Digital Marketing
(Micro Link II)
2670 Cherry Lane
Walnut Creek, California
94596

Teleram
2 Corporate Park Drive
White Plains, New York
10604
914-694-9270